The Visitor's Guide
to
GUERNSEY, ALDERNEY and SARK

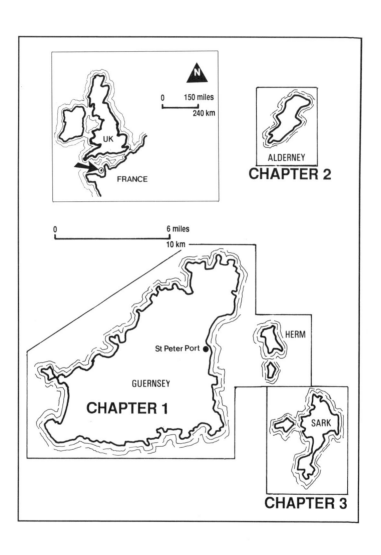

0   150 miles
     240 km

N

UK

FRANCE

ALDERNEY

CHAPTER 2

0   6 miles
                    10 km

St Peter Port

HERM

GUERNSEY

CHAPTER 1

SARK

CHAPTER 3

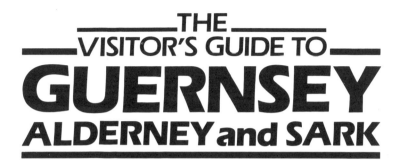

THE VISITOR'S GUIDE TO GUERNSEY ALDERNEY and SARK

Victor Coysh

MPC

INTRODUCTION

O ne of the merits of the Channel Islands is their proximity to the shores of both England and France. It was Victor Hugo (a former Guernsey resident) who wrote that the islands were fragments of France picked up by England and, geographically speaking, he was right. However, since the islands were part of the Duchy of Normandy when Duke William conquered England in l066, it was the Channel Islands, in a sense, who did the picking up!

They lie 75 miles (l20km) south of Weymouth and are within sight of the French coast. The islands have a continental atmosphere which, mingled with a strongly British characteristic, creates an agreeable blend of two worlds. A visitor there goes abroad in Britain, as it were.

The major islands are Jersey, Guernsey, Alderney and Sark, with Herm and Jethou as cherished offspring. The Guernsey Bailiwick includes all of them save Jersey. The word 'Bailiwick' originally meant a region over which a Bailiff had authority. Today the Bailiff of Guernsey is a combination of Lord Chief Justice, Lord Mayor and Speaker in Parliament: his jurisdiction over the smaller islands is minimal. In medieval times the Keeper (Governor) and Bailiff of all the Channel Islands was often one person, so that his jurisdiction was not confined to Guernsey. For centuries, however, there have been

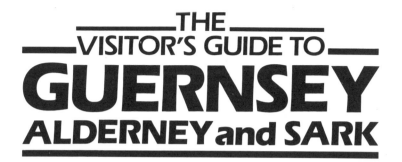

THE VISITOR'S GUIDE TO GUERNSEY ALDERNEY and SARK

Victor Coysh

MPC

Published by:
Moorland Publishing Co Ltd,
Moor Farm Road West,
Ashbourne, Derbyshire DE6 1HD England

Published in the USA by:
Hunter Publishing Inc,
300 Raritan Center Parkway, CN 94,
Edison NJ 08818

ISBN 0 86190 370 6

1st Edition 1983
2nd Edition (fully revised and redesigned) 1989
3rd Edition (revised) 1994

British Library Cataloguing in Publication Data:
A catalogue record for this book is available from the British Library

Colour and black & white origination by: Scantrans, Singapore

Printed in Hong Kong by: Wing King Tong Co Ltd

Front cover: *The Harbour, St Peter Port* (MPC Picture Collection)
Rear cover: *La Seigneurie Gardens, Sark* (MPC Picture Collection)
Illustrations have been supplied as follows; V. Coysh pp:9, 25, 27, 49, 53,
71, 77, 81, 147, 153, 169, 197, 201, 223, 235; All other photographs are
from the MPC Picture Collection.

Acknowledgements
For co-operation in the writing of this book the author is grateful to the
publicity departments of the States of Guernsey, the States of Alderney
and Sark Chief Pleas, the Tenant of Herm (Major Peter Wood), the
Guernsey Press Co Ltd (for permission to use Sark photographs and
map), and to Grut's for the use of some of their photographs.

CONTENTS

Key to Symbols Used on Maps and in Text Margin

 Recommended walk

 Parkland

 Archaeological site

 Nature reserve/Animal interest

 Birdlife

 Garden

 Church/ecclesiastical site

 Building of interest

 Castle/Fortification

 Museum/Art gallery

 Beautiful view/Scenery, Natural phenomenon

 Other place of interest

Note on the maps

The maps drawn for each chapter, while comprehensive, are not designed to be used as route maps, but rather to locate the main towns, villages and places of interest. For exploration, visitors are recommended to use the 1:50,000 (approximately $1\frac{1}{4}$in to the mile) Ordnance Survey 'Landranger' maps. The sheets covering the areas included in this book are shown on the frontispiece. The locally published Perry Guide Maps are also invaluable.

Author's Note

Guernsey localities are named in a mixture of French and English. For instance, Smith Street was originally Rue des Forges and High Street was Grande Rue. In this book, wherever possible, the French version appears on its maps, except in the case of the town streets, most of which, incidentally, carry signs in both languages.

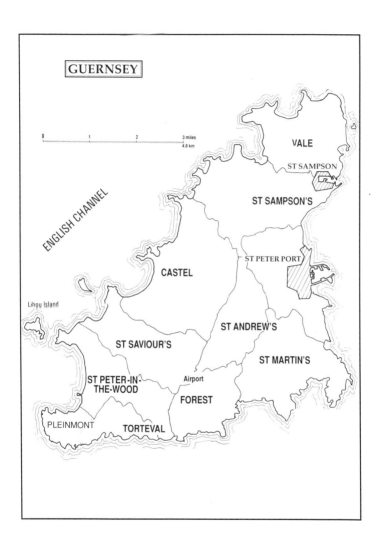

INTRODUCTION

O ne of the merits of the Channel Islands is their proximity to the shores of both England and France. It was Victor Hugo (a former Guernsey resident) who wrote that the islands were fragments of France picked up by England and, geographically speaking, he was right. However, since the islands were part of the Duchy of Normandy when Duke William conquered England in l066, it was the Channel Islands, in a sense, who did the picking up!

They lie 75 miles (l20km) south of Weymouth and are within sight of the French coast. The islands have a continental atmosphere which, mingled with a strongly British characteristic, creates an agreeable blend of two worlds. A visitor there goes abroad in Britain, as it were.

The major islands are Jersey, Guernsey, Alderney and Sark, with Herm and Jethou as cherished offspring. The Guernsey Bailiwick includes all of them save Jersey. The word 'Bailiwick' originally meant a region over which a Bailiff had authority. Today the Bailiff of Guernsey is a combination of Lord Chief Justice, Lord Mayor and Speaker in Parliament: his jurisdiction over the smaller islands is minimal. In medieval times the Keeper (Governor) and Bailiff of all the Channel Islands was often one person, so that his jurisdiction was not confined to Guernsey. For centuries, however, there have been

The rugged coastline of Guernsey

separate Bailiffs of Jersey and Guernsey, each of which has its own States (local government). The term 'Bailiff' persists in the Channel Islands, as do many other ancient expressions.

The Channel Islands are major tourist resorts, but they are not solely dependent on visitors: they are noted for their produce, cattle, fishing and finance corporations. While the visitor is most certainly welcome, he does not feel that his custom alone is necessary for the islands to survive. Rather does he appreciate being a guest in a busy household.

Access to Guernsey is simple. Air services connect it with Britain and elsewhere and one may travel by ferry. The journey across the Channel is relatively brief, yet on arrival in Guernsey one experiences a sensation of agreeable novelty, coupled with the most cordial of welcomes. To borrow a rather well-worn expression, Guernsey is an island that likes to be visited; so do its neighbours.

A feature of these islands is their variety. To travel from Guernsey to Alderney is to experience a change out of all proportion to the score of miles between them. And how unlike each other are Alderney and Sark, even though their size is almost identical! Moreover, each of these islands presents contrasts in its own topography, creating the impression of being in a larger region than is really the case. Every Channel Island is a world in miniature and to explore the group in detail would take a considerable time. Communications between them are frequent and Guernsey's central position simplifies inter-insular travel appreciably.

From the remotest period man has been attracted to the Channel Islands. In Neolithic times he came here to farm in rudimentary fashion and to bury his dead. His massive tombs of granite survive, as do the standing stones he may have worshipped. The islands' archaeological store is abundant and in recent years there have been important discoveries. Despite the destruction of far too many prehistoric monuments the Guernsey Bailiwick still has much to offer both the specialist and layman and these venerable relics of yesterday add greatly to the character of the isles and, surely, to the enjoyment of many who visit them.

Lying off the Normandy coast, they became part of the Duchy and after the Conquest of 1066 they continued to do so, since the King of England remained Duke of Normandy. In 1204, when King John lost his French territories, the islands remained loyal to the Crown and they have remained so to this day. When France became England's enemy, the islands were in peril, for they were dangerously close to their ancient mother country which became, so frequently, their foe.

Despite France's role as a traditional enemy, the long-established associations with it persisted. Under the Norman régime, feudalism flourished and dominated the islanders' way of life. In order to protect his Duchy (which included the Channel Islands) the Duke of Normandy relied upon his subjects. His army was drawn from their ranks and in return they were granted certain privileges. Seigneurs (lords of the manor) were given areas of land (fiefs) which they held

Cows grazing on Herm

in return for either services rendered to the Duke personally or payment in kind. In turn, the Seigneurs granted privileges to those who worked for them, including dwellings and land. The Seigneurs received dues in return, including corn 'rentes', and some of the more important fiefs enjoyed their own manorial courts, thus creating a form of self-government, albeit in miniature.

The Seigneurs originally helped to govern the islands and still pay 'suit of service' to the Royal Court as a form of homage to the Sovereign who, traditionally, holds the islands as Duke of Normandy. Feudalism today scarcely exists, but a number of feudal courts still meet as a matter of tradition, although the ancient dues are no longer paid. Only in Sark does the feudal system remain alive.

Because of the perpetual French threat, Guernsey was fortified to withstand invasion and conquest. To guard St Peter Port and its approaches Castle Cornet was built on an islet offshore and in the north the Vale Castle, probably of later date, protected the entrance to the Little Russel channel. In time, other coastal defences were

GUERNSEY'S SHELTERED BAYS

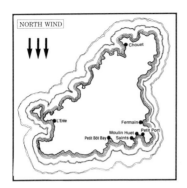

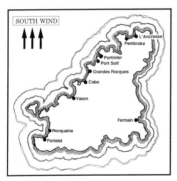

constructed, a garrison was stationed here and the Guernsey Militia was a further insurance against attack. Service in its ranks was compulsory, as in other Channel Island militia forces. Despite these precautions, invasions did occur and in the fourteenth century the French held Castle Cornet for some years.

To the Crown, these islands were worth having. They provided shelter for the English fleet and trading vessels, they occupied a strategic position in the Channel and, had they fallen into French hands, they would have constituted a threat to England. For these reasons they were granted the privilege of home rule, as well as other

These maps show the best bays to visit when the wind is in the direction indicated.

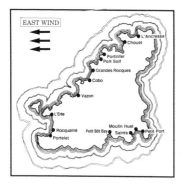

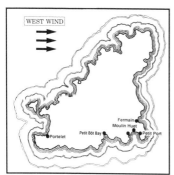

concessions, but while their loyalty to the Crown (rather than to the English Government) remained unshaken, their French origins and associations were never submerged, whether or not they were at war with the French. They bore French place-names (they formed part of the Norman diocese of Coutances until 1568) while the islanders had French names (many still do) and their speech was that of Normandy. The English tongue was foreign to them and if they travelled at all, it was to France rather than to England. Yet in wartime they regarded that country as the enemy. It was a very curious state of affairs which has never been explained satisfactorily.

In the Civil War there was a lapse of loyalty, for while Castle Cornet remained faithful to the king, the rest of Guernsey took the side of Parliament and this resulted in the siege of the castle for nine years. Its garrison was aided by royalist Jersey with men and provisions, and, because of its worth as a guardian fortress, it was not seriously attacked by Parliamentary forces, although from time to time its guns thundered defiance to Guernsey. When the castle ultimately surrendered in 1651, it was the last royalist citadel to do so.

Privateering became a lucrative business to the islanders, since so often England was fighting the French. Local pirates and smugglers also prospered, as well as honest island merchants. Napoleon's efforts to conquer Guernsey failed (although Frenchmen landed in Jersey in 1781 for a few hours until the invaders were driven out), thanks to an English naval squadron based in local waters and a multitude of troops and militia men manning her heavily defended shores.

Napoleon's defeat brought about a major change in the islands' way of life. Warfare gave place to industry (the change, to some, was not financially welcome) and the coming of steam vessels was a boon indeed. Fast and regular passages across the Channel conveyed visitors in one direction and produce in another. A wave of prosperity resulted, something that is still enjoyed. The French influence grew less and English was spoken more freely; yet the distinctive character of these Channel Isles endured. To this day there is a blend of English, French and Guernsey which is wholly agreeable.

World War I left its mark on Guernsey chiefly towards the end of that conflict, when so many former militiamen fell in battle. The years between that war and the next were prosperous. Royalty visited the islands, air travel was inaugurated, major developments were effected, including the enlargement of St Peter Port harbour and the building of an airport far superior to the casual landing place on the west coast.

World War II brought disaster to the Channel Islands when, in 1940, German forces occupied them. While many, children especially, had escaped in time, thousands still remained, apart from Alderney, whose entire population left their homes to settle in Britain. Privations resulted for those who stayed, including the deportation of

A number of Martello towers are to be found on Guernsey

some to Germany. Guernsey and Alderney were turned into fortresses. Heavy artillery, mine fields and massive garrisons made them impregnable and attempts to reconquer would have resulted in immense loss of life and property. So for 5 dreadful years, this part of the United Kingdom was subjected to alien rule. Liberation Day on May 9, 1945, is still observed as an annual holiday in Guernsey.

Whereas Guernsey made a fairly rapid recovery from the German Occupation, it was a different matter for Alderney, where the enemy had wrought massive damage to that uninhabited island. Yet recovery there took place after a few years and today it is more prosperous than it has ever been. As much might be said of Guernsey, whose popularity as a place of residence grew so great in post-war years that the States were obliged to regulate house purchases, in order that newcomers might not oust returning islanders after the Occupation.

Trade has vastly increased since pre-war days. Tourists, yachtsmen, conference delegates, and even Germans who were here under less happy conditions, come to Guernsey and its neighbours by the thousand, by sea and air. Ships take away tomatoes, flowers and visitors determined to return. Banking houses prosper, likewise light industry; cars are almost too numerous for comfort, while a great many houses have been built since 1945. For its size, Guernsey is densely populated. The last census in 1991, revealed a population of 58,873. Alderney had 2,297 inhabitants, Sark had 650, while Herm and Jethou's population was 114, the Bailiwick total being 61,814.

Despite such popularity, the loveliness of these isles in the Channel is imperishable. The cliffs, commons, mighty rocks, sandy bays, crystal-clear waters, the cattle tethered in the meadows, the old country dwellings, the narrow, flower-decked lanes, the splendid harbours, busy marinas and the element of good cheer, prosperity and hospitality are the salient qualities which make the islands the envy of less favoured lands.

Here we find the old and new rubbing shoulders. The golfer passes ancient dolmens as he strides over L'Ancresse Common. The bather is overlooked by many a coastal stronghold. On the cliffs the walker may rest in the shade of an ancient watch-house or maybe by a massive German tower. In St Peter Port aged houses may accommodate boutiques, the venerable Town Church stands beside a busy bus station, while Castle Cornet is the neighbour of anchored yachts. Yesterday and today merge.

There is so much to do in the Channel Islands and yet, for those in need of rest rather than activity, there is abundant peace to be found. One may swim or sunbathe at a score of Guernsey bays and there are miles of superb cliffs for the walker. There is sport in plenty on land and sea. A leisure centre, a cinema and theatres, a wealth of night spots; restaurants and pubs take care of islander and guest alike and bad weather need not mar the holiday. Guernsey's museums are numerous, and quite out of the ordinary; many an interesting old building can be visited, the ancient parish churches are well worth seeing, while the shops are always a magnet.

Prices of many commodities, especially drink, tobacco and perfume, are much lower than elsewhere and the absence of VAT is advantageous. Visit the St Peter Port markets and see what they have to offer. Browse in bookshops and antique shops, lounge in

A Battle of the Flowers exhibit

public gardens and hotel grounds. Study the shipping from the harbour side. Do what you please. You will love Guernsey and her neighbours and will surely wish to return.

To leave Guernsey, temporarily, is simple. Communications with Jersey, Alderney, Sark and Herm are excellent and the fact that Sark and Herm can be visited only by sea is an added attraction, for air travel would surely disturb their tranquility. Inter-island distances are brief. Herm is only 3 miles (nearly 5km) away, Sark is 9 miles (about 14km) from St Peter Port; Jersey and Alderney are approximately 21 miles (about 30km) away.

For those with their own yachts, Guernsey offers four marinas, three at St Peter Port and a fourth near St Sampson's harbour, in the north. Private aircraft, of course, may use the airport. If visitors wish to take their cars to the island they may do so. Alternatively, they may hire a car on the island, or on Alderney.

Everything is made easy for the visitor, with the minimum of fuss and bother. There is an informality about island life which newcomers relish and the blend of continental and English living is a further attraction. These islands are alluring all the year round.

THE GOVERNMENT OF GUERNSEY

The island enjoys home rule and this includes certain privileges, such as the immunity of military service out of the island (waived by Guernsey during the two World Wars), the freedom of island produce from United Kingdom duty, the levying of the island's own duties, the absence of VAT and the ability to make its own laws and generally run its own affairs. The local government, known as the States, comprises the Bailiff (president of the States), twelve Conseillers (elected for 6 years' service), HM Procureur (Attorney-General) and Comptroller (Solicitor-General), thirty-three People's Deputies (equivalent to MPs) and ten Douzaine (parish) representatives. These comprise the States of Deliberation, which meets monthly and includes two representatives of the States of Alderney. Deputies represent the ten island parishes and are elected by public suffrage every 3 years. On the other hand, Conseillers are elected by the States of Election for a 6 years' term of office, while Douzeniers are nominated by their Douzaines (parish councils) to serve for one year. Normally, the Lieutenant-Governor attends States Meetings, but has no vote.

The Royal Court has the Bailiff as its president or, in his absence, the Deputy Bailiff. It comprises twelve Jurats (appointed by the States of Election), the Crown Officers (Procureur and Comptroller), HM Greffier (Clerk), HM Sheriff and HM Sergeant (administrative officers). All wear robes of office. The proceedings are conducted in English, although certain formal utterances are made in French.

The Constitution of the Guernsey Bailiwick, full details of its Government and the history of its constitution and law are admirably explained by Sir John Loveridge, a former Bailiff, in The Constitution and Law of Guernsey obtainable at most island bookshops.

An interesting and most ancient custom, enjoying the full force of law, is Le Clameur de Haro, believed to have originated in the days of William the Conqueror, if not earlier. Here is an example of its modern use: a man may have a tree on his property which, his neighbour alleges, obscures light from his greenhouse. If the owner refuses to fell the tree, his neighbour may decide to do it himself. The

Dolmen on the south-west coast of Guernsey

owner, discovering this course of action, could take the matter to Court, but meanwhile he would have lost his tree. So he has recourse to a form of injunction by 'raising the *Clameur*'. In the presence of two witnesses he falls on his knees and cries, '*Haro, Haro, Haro, a l'aide, mon Prince. On me fait tort* (Help, my Prince, wrong is being done to me)'. This is followed by reciting the Lord's Prayer, in French. On hearing this, the neighbour must stop work at once, or he is liable to a fine for contempt of *Le Clameur*. The tree's owner must then go to the Greffe without delay, formally to register his action. In due course, the case comes before the Court, which decides on the merits of the matter. The virtue of the custom is its summary stay of execution. *Le Clameur* is raised in the Channel Islands fairly frequently.

REGIONAL DIALECTS — PATOIS

Guernsey-French is still spoken locally, but only to a limited degree and chiefly by elderly country people. It is based on the Norman tongue and efforts are constantly being made to keep it alive, by means of classes and books. Despite this, the patois is dying slowly, chiefly because island children very rarely use it, even if they understand this ancient dialect.

Sark-French, again, is mainly spoken by the older generation and most children are unfamiliar with their island language, which has an affinity with Jersey's, as the island was colonised by Jerseymen in the sixteenth century.

Alderney-French is no longer spoken in that island. It was dying out before World War II and the evacuation of the islanders in 1940 killed this brand of patois completely.

GUERNSEY'S FLAG AND ARMS

It is flown from public buildings in the island and from the bonnet of the Bailiff's car (which, incidentally, bears the number I. Unlike the other islands, Guernsey's vehicle number plates bear no prefixes). Officially adopted in 1985, the Guernsey flag comprises the Cross of St George, with the Papal Cross superimposed. For use at sea by local vessels, the Red Ensign carries the Papal Cross in the flag. The flags of Alderney and Sark are similar, though with variations. The former bears a lion rampant in the centre and the latter carries two leopards in the top left-hand corner.

The arms of Guernsey are those of the sovereign. In 1279, Edward I gave Jersey and Guernsey a public seal, in order that the king's own seal need not be used on official island documents. It bore his own arms and these still appear on the Jersey and Guernsey seals, as well as on island coins, and currency notes. The Guernsey seal differs from Jersey's by the addition of a sprig of laurel at the top of the shield, forming a crest.

ISLAND COINS AND STAMPS

Copper or bronze coins have been specially minted for use in Guernsey since 1830. Formerly, they were valued in *doubles*, eight to a penny, four to a halfpenny and two to a farthing. There was also a diminutive *double piece*. All bore the island arms on one face and the value on the other. Until the 1920s French, as well as English, money was legal currency in the islands, to the confusion of the visitor!

With the introduction of decimal coinage, values were in 'new pence' and coins were minted in cupro-nickel. These are in current circulation, although the £1 coin (very small) is unpopular and is rarely seen. Special crown pieces, issued to commemorate auspicious occasions, are not in general circulation. Guernsey currency notes have been in use for very many years and have a distinctive appearance. Local money is not acceptable in the United Kingdom.

Guernsey postage stamps first appeared in 1969 and are esteemed by philatelists. Special issues appear quite often. They, too, must not be used outside the Bailiwick. Details of current and former issues are available from the Philatelic Bureau, at the Post Office in Commercial Arcade, St Peter Port.

1

GUERNSEY

St Peter Port

This, the most ancient town in the Channel Islands, is also the most attractive. Its antiquity, setting and sense of vitality are qualities visitors remember long after other island attractions have faded from the memory. There is an agreeable blend of old and new which, on the whole, pleases the most fastidious and the combination of aged buildings, modern shops, a wealth of diverse entertainment places and, perhaps most important, the remarkable blend of town and harbour lift St Peter Port far above the ordinary.

It has been of importance for centuries. Guernsey was a staging post in the wine trade, when ships bound from England and the Mediterranean used it for shelter and replenishment. Later in its history, wine was laid down here to mature, and to this day several great cellars and vaults serve to remind one of this antique industry.

Doubtless St Peter Port started life as a fishing village. It lacked the physical features to provide a natural harbour, but its roadstead, protected by the nearby islands, attracted mariners and, therefore, traders, and the fishermen were joined by merchants, resulting in the growth of a seaport from a humble fishing haven.

What may once have been a chapel was gradually transformed into what most claim to be the finest church in the Channel Islands

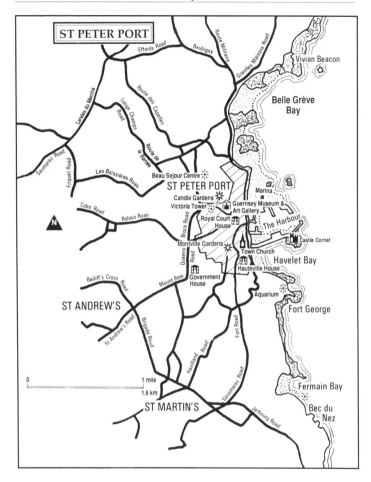

and there is documentary evidence from as early as 1048 confirming its importance as a parish church. The building was gradually enlarged to its present size and old houses which once hemmed it in have been removed to reveal the aged beauty of what every islander calls the '**Town Church**'.

Within this venerable place of worship is an atmosphere of peace, where 'the beauty of holiness' lingers. Its walls are covered with memorials, reminiscent of Westminster Abbey, and much of Guernsey's history can be learned from them. The Colours of the Royal Guernsey Militia hang in the sanctuary and the beautiful Lady Chapel recalls Major-General Sir Isaac Brock, a great Guernseyman who fell in action on a Canadian battlefield in 1812.

The windows of the Town Church are nearly all modern. An explosion in the harbour during the German Occupation destroyed most of the originals, as well as blowing out a great many windows elsewhere. Happily, the replacements are in excellent taste and are generally regarded as superior to the Victorian stained glass. Notice the massive granite masonry of the church and the elegance of the north porch.

Close to the church, almost on the quay, is a stone pillar, known as a *Barrière de la Ville*, one of a number alleged to have marked the sites of gates when the town was walled. In 1350 Edward III ordered this form of defence to be built against the invading French, but confirmation that it was accomplished appears to be lacking and the barrier stones are probably no more than their inscriptions declare: original town boundaries rather than gate sites. Similar stones are to be found at the top of Cornet Street; half-way up Fountain Street at the foot of Rosemary Lane; in Smith Street and opposite Moore's Hotel in Le Pollet.

Next to be explored is **The Harbour**. In the thirteenth century a stone pier was built, running east from the Town Church. It survives as the Albert Pier, but wears a far more sophisticated appearance than it did when small craft berthed along side its rough masonry. The port of St Peter continued to rely on the importance of its roadstead rather than on the primitive jetty until, in the reign of Elizabeth I, the pier was improved and, when Anne was queen, the north pier was built. Both enclose what used to be known as the Old Harbour, though today they embrace the Victoria and Albert yacht marinas, retaining names given to the piers following the visit of Queen Victoria and Prince Albert in the last century.

What used to be styled the New Harbour is a Victorian master-piece in stone, constructed because of the inadequacy of the original port, which dried out at low tide, was of small area and incapable of accommodating ships of appreciable tonnage. The vastly larger New

Commercial Arcade, St Peter Port

Harbour embraced within its granite arms the ancient pile of Castle Cornet, formerly sited on an islet. A harbour arm sprang from the South Esplanade (where the bus station is), passed the castle and terminated in a massive breakwater, whose extremity was graced by a comely lighthouse. Another, across the pierheads to the north, guides the sailor into the haven's safety.

An important appendix to St Peter Port was built in the 1920s. Known as the Jetty, it is unlovely in concrete, yet is of the greatest use in providing berths for ferries, cargo and fishing vessels as well as roll-on roll-off ramps for vehicles. There are spacious offices and waiting rooms, on whose flat roofs one may observe the life of the port. On both the upper walks of its northern and southern arms there are similar vantage points, with seats for comfort. Here, in the evening, anglers frequently gather. Notice, on St Julian's Pier, the memorial to the twenty-nine islanders who were killed when the Germans launched an air raid on Guernsey just prior to the Occupation.

Unhappily, Guernsey has a vast vehicle population and parking spaces are inadequate. Multi-storey car parks are unlovely but valuable, and before long the island may well have them, in, it is hoped, inconspicuous corners. Meanwhile, the harbour wharves serve as parking places and the pedestrian is well advised to walk above them. The Queen Elizabeth II marina has pontoon moorings for about 800 craft, 10 deep-water berths and parking for over 1,000 vehicles.

TOWN TOUR 1

St Peter Port's parish church adjoins the bus station (whose enquiry and tours offices are at the nearby Picquet House, formerly used by the military) and one or two car parks are to be found here. It is, therefore, an ideal starting place for a walk round the town centre (the only worthwhile way of exploring it). Narrow, one-way streets make driving there an abomination and to enjoy the town is to stroll through it. Pedestrian precincts make this additionally agreeable.

Firstly, wander, then, up **High Street**, noticing its ancient paving. Until about 60 years ago many of the town's ways were paved thus, but unfortunately several were subsequently given modern surfaces; High Street, Le Pollet, Contrée Mansell (in the western regions) and

Vegetable Market, St Peter Port

various lanes to be explored later retain their traditional paving stones.

The shops of the town are, for the most part, filled with such good things that most visitors look harder at their window displays than at

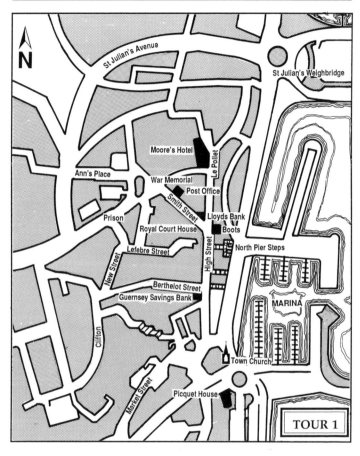

their architecture. This is a pity, for several are finely proportioned and are a reminder of the fact that, up to some 150 years ago, they were the town houses of wealthy Guernseymen. Road surfaces, then, were bad and in winter almost impassable, so the gentry elected to reside either in their country seats or their town residences, refraining from commuting unless it was really necessary. The fact that, in a small island, distances between the most remote dwellings and the town were but a few miles did not deter the opulent from having a *pied-à- terre* in either camp, so to speak.

*Side street,
St Peter Port*

Modern shopfronts have scarcely improved the façades of St Peter Port's buildings and very few retain their former fair frontages. However, apart from a small number of blatant examples of bad taste, most of the shopfronts blend tolerably well with the more antique parts of the buildings, thanks, in part, to the vigilance of the States Island Development Committee, an official body which judges the merits of alterations made to the fabric of any building, old or modern, as well as casting a critical eye on all new construction. In this way, much of the town and countryside looks better than would have been the case had the IDC not existed, although naturally any eyesores built before the committee was formed are allowed to remain.

Wealth accumulated as a result of privateering and other, more mercantile, ventures and this produced changes in medieval St Peter Port. Humble dwellings often became rich folk's town houses, improved roads brought more country people to market, shops became more numerous and the town expanded. In 1742 a hospital was built for the indigent and old, and in 1811 the island prison ceased to be at Castle Cornet. Its successor was built in St James's Street, with a subway linking it with the Royal Court House. The prison is now at Les Nicolles, St Sampson's. St Peter Port Hospital is nearby.

In the 1830s the **Commercial Arcades** were constructed between the Market Square and the middle of High Street. These were Guernsey's first pedestrian precincts. Their buildings have flat roofs, since the Arcades were to have had a glass covering, but the money ran out and they remain open to the weather. Nevertheless, they are both attractive and useful. The introduction of street lighting by gas further improved the town at this period.

Half-way up High Street and just beyond the Arcades' entrance, is the Guernsey Savings Bank, a house still retaining something of its medieval aspect, at least on the outside. The merchant marks of Jean Briard may be discerned on its stone 'jetties'. Close by is Berthelot Street (very steep), where more old buildings will be seen in a thoroughfare of much charm. It leads to Clifton, part of an area of elegant Georgian houses from which fine views seaward are to be enjoyed — some reward, perhaps, for the effort of reaching them from the town.

On the right of High Street, as one ascends, are two insignificant openings, known as *venelles*. One faces Berthelot Street and the other adjoins the National Westminster Bank. They provide quick access to the quayside, like the third, at the top of the street. This is more conspicuous and is known as the North Pier Steps, from which intriguing lesser flights to right and left are worth exploring.

Opposite the top of these steps is an archway, leading to Lefebvre Street, another steep hill running to Clifton. In a small square stands **Le Manoir Le Marchant**, an admirable house of great age, now used as offices by the Constables of St Peter Port. In Guernsey a Constable is an important parochial officer and not just a policeman! Each parish has two and they are roughly equivalent to mayors.

The town, fortunately, continues to display its old street names, as well as the modern ones, and the top of High Street is still proclaimed *Le Grand Carrefour*, the great crossroads. This rather

The first post box in Guernsey

ambitious expression denotes the meeting of High Street, Smith Street, Le Pollet and the Pier Steps. Here stands Boots' premises, with its stately granite facade, bearing a plaque stating that Sir Isaac Brock once lived there.

Straight on, past the fine green dome of Lloyds Bank, is **Le Pollet** (the Pollet to islanders and Pollet Street to visitors), an old cobbled way leading northward to the seashore. Aged buildings flank it and some of those on the east side are of great antiquity. Indeed, cannon balls have been found there, shot from Castle Cornet during the Civil War. Fortunately, the Pollet has many small shops, a harmonious complement to the narrow street and a reminder of how it used to be when the town comprised only a handful of such thoroughfares. Moore's Hotel, once a town residence of the de Saumarez family and still looking like it, faces a shop bearing a plaque. It proclaims the fact

PLACES OF INTEREST IN AND AROUND ST PETER PORT

Aquarium
La Vallette.
Housed in former tunnel. Local and tropical fish, shellfish and reptiles. Open daily.

Bathing Pools
La Vallette.
Facilities for swimming and diving. Refreshments. Attractive gardens adjoining. Path to Clarence Battery and Fort George above Aquarium.

Beau Sejour Leisure Centre
Amherst.
Set in spacious grounds. Free parking. All manner of outdoor and indoor amusements, including swimming, squash, tennis, badminton, theatre, bars, restaurant. Open throughout the year. Occasional exhibitions and conferences.

Castle Cornet
Open daily, April-October.

Splendid collection of Channel Islands Militia uniforms, badges, silver etc, also Castle Museum with British Army and German objects on display. Works of art. Excellent Maritime Museum. Guided tours of castle. Noonday gun fired. Castle within easy walking distance of the town. Parking nearby.

Fermain Bay
Popular and beautiful. Boat from St Peter Port. (*Bus Al, A2*), with walk down valley to beach. Refreshments.

Guernsey Museum & Art Gallery
Candie Gardens.
Open daily. Houses selection of archaeological and historical exhibits including pictures and ceramics. Audio visual theatre. Frequent special exhibitions. Refreshments in former bandstand.

that Sir Edgar MacCulloch, a former Bailiff, once lived there. He was the founder of La Société Guernesiaise, the island's learned society which celebrated its centenary in 1982.

For its neighbour Le Pollet has La Plaiderie ('the place of pleading'). Here stood the Royal Court House, whose paving stones and granite steps are all that remain of its former glory, though this building bears small resemblance to the far more dignified successor up the hill. Continuing along a narrow footpath, you will reach Le

Guernsey Toys
Victoria Road.
Visitors may watch them being
made.

Hauteville House
Hauteville.
Victor Hugo's home, 1856-70.
Many personal possessions of
the poet displayed, works of art,
tapestries, valuable furniture,
china etc. His rooftop study has
a glorious view. Open daily, but
number of visitors at any one
time is limited, so it is as well to
go early to avoid a long wait.
Parking is difficult near the
house.

Munson Gallery
North Pier Steps.
Open daily.

**Notre Dame du Rosaire
Church**
Burnt Lane, off Mill Street.
Roof like upturned boat.
Wonderfully restored. Musical
festival during summer. Tucked
away but well worth finding.

Priaulx Library
Candie Road.
Open daily. Comprehensive
collection of Channel Islands
books, maps and papers among
its treasures.

St James's Picture Gallery
Tudor House, Bordage.
Open daily.

Town Church
Rated finest in the Channel
Islands. Medieval architecture,
modern glass, Colours and
historic memorials.

Underground Military Museum
La Vallette
Interesting Occupation and
garrison relics in tunnel which
formerly housed the fuel tanks of
German U-boats.

Victoria Tower
Monument Gardens.
Key at Fire Station, opposite.

Truchot, a modernised road leading to the seafront. It is better
approached via the Lower Pollet, which has more fascinating shops
and restaurants.

The street ends at La Tourgand, an area in which once stood a
medieval tower, guarding the town's northern approaches. Here is St
Julian's Weighbridge, an attractive stone building with a clock tower.
It is a busy place for traffic and the walker is advised to proceed up
leafy St Julian's Avenue (with traffic lights at its foot), and, further up,

The Harbour, St Peter Port

there is a charming little garden in which stands an unconventional monument: a soldier standing guard over his wounded comrade. It commemorates islanders who fell in the South African War.

 At the top of the Avenue turn left and enter Ann's Place. Soon you will pass one of Guernsey's finest hotels, the former Government House, facing a rather curious sunken garden. Here once stood St Paul's Methodist Church, demolished in 1972, which replaced La Maison Carré, once the town residence of Admiral Lord de Saumarez.

 Across the way in Rue du Manoir is the **Royal Court House**, built in 1799 and well worth viewing. It houses the Greffe (where interesting public records are kept) and, upstairs, the Royal Court Chamber, elegantly appointed. Here important trials take place and it is also the venue of the States of Deliberation (the island parliament), whose monthly meetings are interesting. At the rear of the Court House is the former Prison, opposite the unusually designed and disused Church of St James the Less, now an ornate and very successful concert hall.

 The **Island War Memorial**, with its figures of St George and the dragon, stands between Old Government House Hotel and the Court House; downhill is Smith Street, once known as La Rue des Forges (street of the farriers), wider than most in the town and lacking antiquity in appearance; its shopfronts are modern, although those of Messrs Lovell and Gillow are extremely elegant.

 In an open space stands one of the town's pumps. Once common, only a few now remain. A flight of steps leads up to Le Marchant Street and at the top is Rue du Manoir. Turn left to reach the top of Lefebvre Street, beyond which is New Street, leading to the summit of Berthelot Street. Near this point is the citadel of the Salvation Army, and a flight of steps beside it descends to Market Street.

TOWN TOUR 2

Starting again from the church, walk up Fountain Street, passing shops on the left and the large **Market House** on the right. The fish, meat, vegetable and flower markets are very well worth seeing and, while most visitors gaze intently at the attractive wares, they should also spare a glance at the lofty arches, roofs, stone-work and the

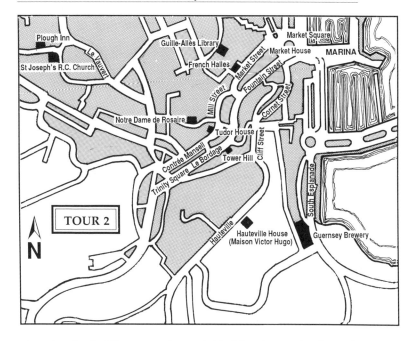

almost cathedral-like proportions of this Victorian work of art. Of special appeal is the array of shellfish (some alive) and, even more appealing, the superb splash of colour in the flower market. No longer, alas, are roasted chestnuts sold there, as they were earlier in the century.

And very seldom seen in the fish market nowadays is the ormer, that savoury 'sea ear' (so called because of its shape), housed in a mother-of- pearl shell. It has a distinctive flavour, but popular though it is, especially among islanders, ormers may only be taken on a few days annually and even then catches are small, as their stocks are depleted. This mollusc, peculiar to the Channel Islands, clings to rocks well below low water mark and to find them is a laborious business, as is their preparation and cooking. The flesh is not unlike a veal cutlet in flavour and the shell is prized as an ashtray or as a form of decoration. It is illegal to dive for them and offenders are prosecuted.

St Peter Port Church on the seafront

The Harbour, St Peter Port

On the return to Fountain Street, Le Petit Carrefour is reached, while on the left is **Le Bordage**, an interesting old street, despite much modern development. The gentle hill leads to the triangular Trinity Square. Here stands **Holy Trinity Church**, built in 1789 and of no great appeal externally, although its recently restored interior well repays a visit. Hereabout are many fascinating places, including an old pub, and antique shops. To wander through the adjacent Contrée Mansell, Mansell and Mill Streets is to obtain a glimpse of how St Peter Port must have looked a century ago. Beyond the square is Rue du Pre and La Charroterie, where there is an extensive business complex.

Mansell Street leads down to Mill Street, with the big Tudor House complex. It is flanked by steps named Ruette Marie Gibault and opposite them are more steps, known as Burnt Lane. It is worth exploring. After passing a school one reaches the church of **Notre Dame du Rosaire**, originally built in 1829 and reconstructed in 1962. Its roof resembles an upturned boat. Although this Roman Catholic church may be modern, the good taste shown in its restoration is admirable and this applies in equal measure to the slim and elegant belfry at its elbow.

Leaving Notre Dame, turn right and then left and stroll up Vauvert until the Plough Inn is reached. Opposite is a steep little lane, popularly and mysteriously known as the 'Cat's Ladder', which leads to St Joseph's Roman Catholic Church, designed by Pugin in 1851. Its handsome spire was added in 1885. Having inspected the church, bear right, turn left, then right to the top of Vauvert. Pass its school on the left and descend the hill to Contrée Mansell.

Such a perambulation through St Peter Port must sometimes involve retracing one's steps, though this is no hardship. Mill Street brings you down to Market Street, where the greatest attraction is the **French Halles**, a covered market, finely arched and ablaze with colourful fruit and flowers. Above is the **Guille-Allès Library**, once the Assembly Rooms and almost rebuilt in the 1970s. The result is extremely satisfactory and this free library (as it has become) is one of the most stately of St Peter Port's public buildings. It looks across to Les Arcades, and its shops and paved walk create a pleasing effect. Market Square is little more than a car park, except on

Flower bedecked shop in a side street of St Peter Port

Thursday afternoons in summer. Then an open market is held again (as was the case before the covered markets were built) and this display, chiefly for the benefit of visitors, makes the place very merry and bright.

From the Town Church a steep hill, Cornet Street, runs southward. Within living memory this was architecturally attractive, with ancient houses on either side, but it was also a slum and in the interest of hygiene much of its western border was demolished. A goodly plantation and masonry replace the dwellings, and Rosemary Lane wavers over the hillside, ultimately taking one across to

St Peter Port

*Boats moored in
St Peter Port Harbour*

Fountain Street. Half-way up Cornet Street is an interesting old shop,
now the headquarters of the National Trust of Guernsey, well
restored after years of neglect.

At the summit of Cornet Street is the former St Barnabas' Church,
built in 1874 and becoming redundant in the 1920s. For a time it was
a museum and now, derelict, its future is doubtful. Were it to be
demolished its fine tower would be missed and the striking skyline of
St Peter Port, best seen from the harbour, would be poorer. Below the
building a broad flight of steps descends to the Bordage and there is
also an alternative approach via Tower Hill, whose name recalls Tour
Beauregard, the fellow of Tour Gand in the north.

Close to the site of this, the former southern defence work of the
town, Cliff Street plunges downhill to the South Esplanade. On the
way it merges into flights of steps, but an alternative route to the coast

is via the Strand, running from Cliff Street to La Vallette. Another variation is Coupée Lane, on the left of Cliff Street, leading to Cornet Street.

But walk up **Hauteville**, one of St Peter Port's most attractive quarters, climbing south from St Barnabas'. It begins humbly enough, with old and rather pleasant buildings on either hand. As the hill becomes steep, the houses become grander and, while many today are private hotels, their exterior nobility has, for the most part, been retained. The best known of them is solemn-faced **Hauteville** **House**, the residence of Victor Hugo from 1855 to 1870, when he voluntarily exiled himself from France for political reasons.From his roof-top study he wrote some of his finest work and enjoyed a panorama unmatched in Guernsey. The house, now owned by La Ville de Paris, is open to the public and should be visited.

At the top of Hauteville turn left and enter Havelet, a lovely road winding down to the sea. It is very narrow at first and then it widens, with gaps between the attractive houses (some of them now hotels) to permit enchanting glimpses of the waterfront. Some especially decorative dwellings adorn the right-hand side of Havelet, as it winds downwards, and there is a fine, wooded estate, too. At the hill's foot stands the Guernsey Brewery. Much less than a quarter of a mile ahead is the bus terminus.

TOWN TOUR 3

Stroll along the quayside, glancing at the mass of yachts (of several nationalities) in the marina. On the left, old, lofty buildings flank the road, most of them with modern frontages. The largest is by no means the most handsome; indeed, the reverse is the case. One which retains much of its former character is Marquand's ship chandlery, where all manner of nautical gear is obtainable in an appropriate atmosphere. Close by are the North Pier Steps and the local headquarters of the Royal Channel Islands Yacht Club.

Walking past the grey granite States Offices and a colourful plantation, the Weighbridge is reached, a busy centre. The Royal Hotel lies ahead, one of the biggest in Guernsey, whose centrepiece, once styled Le Grand Bosq (The Big Wood) was originally one of St Peter Port's town houses. Just past the hotel is Bosq Lane, which

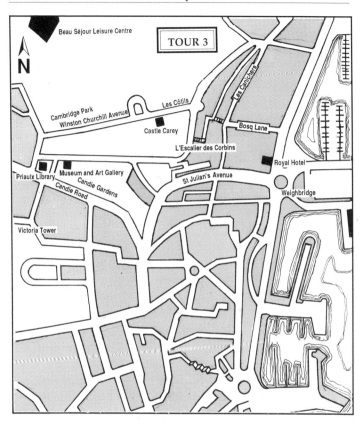

leads to Les Canichers, an old, strange-looking street running from St Julian's Avenue to the suburb of St John's.

Across this road is a long flight of steps, L'Escalier des Corbins, which looks rather daunting. Still, the climb is eased by stretches of level pathway and the view at the top is compensation indeed. This is **Les Côtils** (Steep Slopes), where a 'belvedere' has been built, complete with seats and a helpful 'view finder', explaining what is visible in clear weather.

A steep hill plunges down to St John's, but a walk upwards for a short distance passes **Castle Carey** on the left and Les Côtils estate opposite. The former is not really a castle but an imposing nineteenth-

Looking towards St Peter Port from Castle Cornet

century mansion set in a lovely garden and enjoying a wide outlook. The latter was originally a large dwelling in an engaging park.

Just beyond it is **Cambridge Park**, where games are played and children scramble over a pensioned-off steam roller, among other diversions. In the Winston Churchill Avenue is a reminder that here the last duel in Guernsey was fought. The park was once called the New Ground, whose dull title was changed after the Duke of Cambridge visited the island (and Castle Carey) about a century ago. Its neighbour is the **Beau Sejour Leisure Centre**, whose complex replaces a fine old house. Happily, it retains gracious grounds where various sports are to be enjoyed. The centre has a great deal to offer the visitor, on fine days or foul, including a theatre, cinema, swimming pool, indoor sporting facilities, food and drink. Conferences are sometimes held there.

It is a good idea to return to the western end of Cambridge Park, by the massive Duke of Richmond Hotel and make for **Victoria Tower**, 100ft high, mighty to behold in its splendid red stone and

Candie Gardens

forming a substantial commemoration of the Queen's visit in 1846. It can be climbed (the key is kept at the fire station opposite) and the wide prospect from the top is extensive. In the gardens below the tower are two German guns, relics of World War I. Believing their presence might prove tactless when the Germans arrived in 1940, the guns were hurriedly buried and only resurrected after Liberation Day.

On returning to Candie Road (which was crossed between the park and the tower) the Priaulx Library can be seen. It has an excellent collection of local books (among others), which are avail- able for all to consult. Adjacent are **Candie Gardens**, certainly worth visiting, especially the lower grounds. They are relatively small and are sheltered by mellow walls and abound in colourful trees, shrubs and flowers, some of them rarities. Goldfish swim in the former duckponds, birds sing and an air of peace prevails.

In the upper gardens are two statues: Queen Victoria looks eastward, as does Victor Hugo, a little further away. The former is conventional; the latter is especially fine, for it depicts the poet standing on a mass of granite, gazing at distant France. Nearby once stood a bandstand, where musicians of the garrison and the Royal Guernsey Militia gave concerts and where other entertainments were provided.

The bandstand is now an adjunct to that great Guernsey attraction, the Museum and Art Gallery, a modern home for the treasures of the past. It houses a selection of pieces removed from the former Lukis and Island Museum at the top of Cornet Street, and the displays are changed occasionally. The arrangement, on modern lines, has, as a further attraction, an audio-vision theatre. Exhibitions are held throughout the year. Adjoining it is the headquarters of *La Société Guernesiaise*, the island's 'learned society'.

Down the hill one arrives at the top of St Julian's Avenue, which can also be gained, further down, if one uses the exit from Candie's lower grounds. Crossing the road to Ann's Place and Old Government House Hotel, one can return to the town.

TOWN TOUR 4

Because St Peter Port is built on a hill, a certain amount of climbing

Firing the Noonday Gun, Castle Cornet

is unavoidable if the town is to be seen thoroughly. The town's upper regions can be reached by road also and it is a good idea to proceed thus in an upward direction and descend by the steps, admiring the seascape en route.

All these tours of the town cover quite a small area and it entails no great effort to enjoy them. Of course, they can be curtailed at will. One which certainly ought not to be missed is the walk to Castle Cornet and La Vallette. Both are within easy distance of the town centre and of each other, and the contrast between them is part of their attraction. From the Town Church the way lies southward, passing the Albert Marina on the left and the bus station and shops on the other hand. Notice the statue of the Prince Consort, high above the traffic.

Castle Cornet cannot be missed as the left-hand turn goes along the southern arm of the harbour. Along here is the Model Yacht Pond, a Victorian structure used rather less than formerly. In the vicinity are laid-up boats and the possible destruction of the pond would permit more to stay there during the winter. During World War I the pond was the site of a French naval seaplane base and in World War II it was again destroyed and the Germans fortified the area, as they did

Castle Cornet

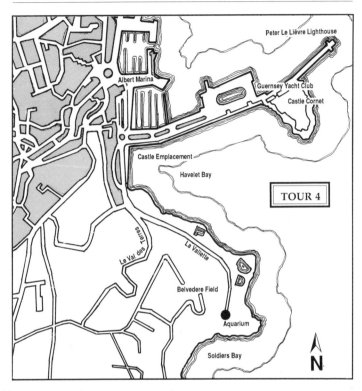

Castle Cornet. Near the headquarters of the Guernsey Yacht Club is a German bunker.

The ancient fortress looked more impressive when it was isolated and, even more so, when its keep was intact, prior to an explosion in 1672. Yet it is still a fine stronghold and if some of its architectural features have gone, always remember that it was a fortress from the time of its building in the thirteenth century to the German Occupation. During that time it was a place of defence, rather than a tourist attraction. King George VI presented it to the people of Guernsey in 1945.

Because of its continuous use by the military over the centuries, changes in its architecture have been inevitable, yet sufficient remains of the medieval castle to reveal its antiquity. There are

Items on show in the Militia Museum, Castle Cornet

guided tours, or one may wander around at will. Notice the row of cannon opposite the Guardhouse, where the RAF Museum is worth seeing. Close by is the Main Guard, a large building housing collections of pictures, relics of the Occupation and more. A short distance further, beyond a flight of steps, a gun is fired with ceremony at noon on weekdays. Nearby is the excellent maritime museum.

At this level is the magnificent Militia Museum, with its unrivalled array of old uniforms and other martial regalia. See the armoury and, in utter contrast, admire the flowers which relieve the scene from the severity of the ramparts. Climb more steps to the Cavalier Battery, on the castle's crown and look around at the wide prospect of sea and islands. Even the less historically-minded will surely enjoy Castle Cornet, if only for the views it commands. Refreshments are served in the imposing Refectory, formerly married quarters.

Leaving this former guardian of Guernsey, a pleasant stroll is to

A quiet corner of Castle Cornet

Castle Cornet

continue to the end of the breakwater, where Peter le Lièvre's lighthouse stands. This eminent Guernsey artist's drawings and paintings are in the castle. From the breakwater's end look landward towards St Peter Port. Its old houses huddle beside the harbour, others climb the hill and at the summit stand the towers of St Barnabas', Elizabeth College, St James' and Victoria Tower, among others. Those who come to Guernsey by ship enjoy this fine prospect, especially at early morning, when the rising sun illuminates a thousand windows.

To reach **La Vallette** return along the harbour, turning left at the slaughter house (beautifully built in red granite) and walk beside Havelet Bay. At the brewery, on leaving Havelet, follow the coast to enter the region of La Vallette. On the right, raised above the road and below masses of trees, are particularly beautiful gardens, with cliffs rising steeply to the former Fort George, now a housing estate. On the left are four swimming pools, and more gardens bordering the sea. There is an abundance of seats, refreshments are available and here you may spend a pleasant hour or two, watching the swimmers and divers and perhaps joining them. Nearly opposite the first pool is La Vallette Underground Military Museum which is well worth a visit.

Close by is the **Aquarium**, not to be missed. It is within a tunnel and a path climbs above it to **Clarence Battery**, an outlier of Fort George and an excellent viewpoint. A little further uphill is a path leading to **Soldiers' Bay** (Petit Fort Bay really), where once the military bathed. It is pleasantly sheltered and from the beach one may see the launch plying between St Peter Port and Fermain Bay.

The really energetic will continue up the hill to **Belvedere Field**, where military parades were once held. Here, again, the view is vast. Guernsey, indeed, is the place for extensive panoramas, interesting and ever-changing, according to the time of day and the vagaries of weather. Fort George lost nearly all its martial aspects when civilians captured the stronghold, but the Main Barrier Gate still stands, west of Belvedere. Pass through it and then turn right.

This is **Le Val des Terres**, one of Guernsey's loveliest roads, opened by the Prince of Wales (the future Edward VIII) in 1935. An inscribed stone in French at the top records the fact. Le Val, with trees on either hand, winds downhill, the heights of the fort on the right, and it emerges at the foot of Havelet. This journey's end is just ahead.

TOWN TOUR 5

A walk through the town thoroughfares westward via St James's Street leads to **Elizabeth College**, large and ancient (for Elizabeth was its foundress in 1563), although the present pseudo-Tudor building dates from 1826. The Lower School is in the Queen's Road and its playing fields are in King's Road and Foote's Lane, on the way to Cobo. The college's neighbours in Grange Road are stately. Equally impressive are the buildings of New Town, a region south of Grange Road, and the same may be said of those in the Queen's Road, adjacent, where **Government House** stands. The Union flag flies there when His Excellency the Lieutenant-Governor is in residence.

Mount Row, just beyond, has an especially lovely field adjoining one of its houses. At its western end is **Le Vauquiedor**, a wooded valley where, on the one hand, is the relatively vast Princess

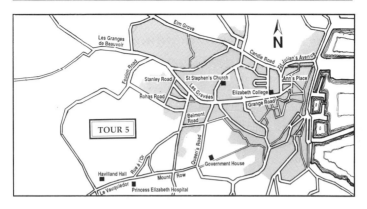

Elizabeth Hospital and on the other **Havilland Hall**, gracious, standing in fine grounds and formerly the home of the Blüchers, once tenants of Herm. Almost beside its gates is Rue à l'Or, a pretty rural lane, running back to Queen's Road via Belmont Road. Where Queen's Road joins Grange Road, turn left, along Les Gravées, the site of more impressive houses, some now hotels, with the Ladies' College a prominent feature.

    St Stephen's Church, of Victorian origin, is well worth a visit; its interior is spacious and beautiful. Further down the road is a remarkably fine old double archway, popularly known as the Ivy Gates, leading to Les Granges de Beauvoir, one of the oldest dwellings in St Peter Port. It is near Stanley Road, leading to Route Isabelle, from which Les Granges can be seen. At the foot of this road is **Le Foulon cemetery** and crematorium. Here lie the remains of sailors lost and washed ashore when HMS *Charybdis* and *Limbourn* were sunk in World War II, off St Malo. Annually the event is marked by a memorial service, moving and full of quiet pageantry, attended by men of the Royal Navy and Royal Marines, local dignitaries and many others.

    At the lower end of the cemetery, at the foot of the hill leading to the crematorium, is a lively duck pond, and an archway, with handsome gates, adorns the main entrance to the burial ground. Foulon Road, practically opposite, runs up to Rohais Road and, bearing right, one returns to Les Granges' archways. Opposite, a

Fermain Bay

short length of road leads to La Gibauderie, running downhill and then upwards to Elm Grove. This continues to Candie Road, lined by several dignified dwellings. The way goes past Candie Gardens and descends to the top of St Julian's Avenue, where Ann's Place leads back to the town. On the way deviate down Hirzel Street (at the top of Smith Street) and see another grand stone archway, the entrance of the former St Peter Port Hospital, near the Island Police Station.

St Peter Port Byways

By no means is St Peter Port an urban parish for, like its fellows, there are rural aspects to be enjoyed. Nor are its suburbs to be despised, and it is through some of them that the visitor may take a walk or two. Set out westward to Trinity Square and continue up Rue du Pre and La Charroterie (The Place of Wagons) to the foot of Colborne Road, where three roads meet. Close by are the recently built State Offices.

 A short distance uphill is an ornate-looking building on the left, with a coat of arms on its façade. It is the escutcheon of the Priaulx family who owned the Montville estate, of which this house was the lodge. Stroll through this property, open to the public and known as **Montville Gardens**. Few seem to use it, yet it is peaceful, not without charm and affording unusual glimpses of the town below. It ends, all too soon, half-way up Les Vardes, a steep hill extending from the top of Hauteville. Where Montville Drive joins the road Montville House stood, until it was destroyed by lightning in 1911. Just below its site, on the left, Park Lane steps descend to Rue du Pré, near the Victoria Homes for the elderly.

 Continue up Les Vardes where the road soon becomes level and joins Colborne Road. Cross here and enter the semi-rural Havilland Road. On the right is the ancient Havilland House and its younger neighbours. The road forks and the right-hand branch leads down to the pleasant Havilland Vale. Further on is the region of Les Hubits, once a place of farms and fields, but now more suburban, although still agreeable.

 At the top of the hill is Green Acres Hotel and the lane (Les Traudes) passes it in a southerly direction. Soon St Martin's Church spire will be seen and La Bellieuse is reached, the lovely settlement in the shadow of the church. A very short distance ahead is **Grande Rue**, St Martin's shopping centre, where a bus may be taken back to town. Alternatively the walker may return by another, equally pleasant, route.

Having looked at the parish church and the old houses (described in more detail later), visitors should retrace their steps until a right-hand turn is reached, which becomes Les Blanches Pierres Lane; take this, passing a football pitch en route. Continue, ignoring a left-hand turning and you will reach the settlement of **Les Hubits de Bas**, with several nice old houses to admire. Here, at the boundary of St Martin's and St Peter Port, is a handsome fountain, with an inscription on its dressed granite.

A stone's throw ahead is the Fort Road and the bus route, but why not walk a mile or so further? Opposite the fountain are Les Damouettes Lanes, running north, and again they are pleasant to follow. Before long they join Havilland Road (at its junction with Havilland Vale) and the return to town may then be made via Colborne Road or Les Vardes. A third alternative is to turn right at the junction and at the top of the hill descend George Road, on the left. This leads to Hauteville and the town.

Rural St Peter Port can be visited by bus (*Bus G*) to Les Baissières (alight at Friquet junction) and from there walk west to another junction, and turn right, past the Butterfly Farm at Le Friquet. The road continues to Rue Cohu (where a fine double archway should be inspected) and then turn right once more, heading towards Les Landes Methodist Church. Then walk along Les Landes du Marché (rather busy) until a crossroads is gained, then turn right along Longue Rue and into Les Canus road. Where this joins Route des Capelles, there is a bus stop.

Had one alighted from the bus at St Peter Port School on the previous walk one could have varied it by seeing the fields, usually full of Guernsey cattle, at La Ramée. Skirt the school, pass a housing estate and walk along Skin's Lane, near which are playing fields. This runs into Neuve Rue, running northward and a right-hand turn leads into Route de la Ramée. One may continue northwards to reach Les Capelles (where there are buses), but it is preferable to go south and

Bec du Nez, a fishing haven below Fermain Bay

follow this country road to La Couture. The farms and cattle are a reminder of the time when the town of St Peter Port was but a fragment of the parish.

At La Couture are traffic lights and just short of them, on approaching the crossroads, there is a right-hand turning. This is the start of the Couture water lanes, a very pleasant locality reserved for pedestrians. All too soon they join Les Ozouets Road and St Peter Port School lies ahead. A bus back to town rounds off this excursion; but there is an alternative for the tireless pedestrian. One may retrace one's steps beside the stream, turn right to the traffic lights and then left. Pass the **Caledonia Nursery** (worth seeing) and, walking up Fosse André, reach the Beau Sejour region. A bus can be taken to the town, although the walk, mostly downhill, is to be recommended.

SOUTH COAST CRUISE

On most summer afternoons Herm Seaways run a delightful cruise along much of Guernsey's southern shores, affording close views of the cliffs, revealing aspects invisible from the land. The launch leaves St Peter Port either from the Town Church slipway or the Albert Pier (according to tidal conditions) and threads her way through the multitude of yachts before passing through the pierheads. She turns to starboard and one can gaze up at Castle Cornet's ramparts before skirting Havelet Bay, with its anchored craft, swimming pools and tree-filled heights.

The route passes close to Clarence Battery and Soldiers' Bay, with the houses of Fort George high above. The cliffs are well wooded, with the buildings of Village de Putron appearing as the boat sails southwards, passing a landing place and steps on the way. Fermain Point lies ahead and, rounding it, is the beautiful **Fermain Bay**, and from the sea one can gaze into its deep, clear water in which the greenery of the cliffs is reflected. Boats often anchor here, among them the launch which runs a regular service between St Peter Port and this favourite beach.

Across Fermain is the fishing haven of **Bec du Nez** and beyond is the Pine Forest, with **Pied du Mur** (Marble Bay) below it. Rocks, cliffs, vegetation, deep waters, seabirds and passing craft enrich the scene, as the launch forges ahead towards St Martin's Point. As the

Cunard's Vistafjord, *one of the many large cruise liners visiting Guernsey seen here anchored outside St Peter Port harbour*

boat skims past the lighthouse **Telegraph Bay** may be noticed *en passant*. The cliffs begin to lose their wooded, gentle, look and become grander and more rugged.

The launch hugs the fretted coast, with its savage rocks and daunting heights. The **Peastacks** tower above; only from the sea can their true majesty be gauged. Gulls wheel above the stacks as the boat passes them by, bound for **Petit Port**. Should the tide be low its broad sands will be seen, above which are the huge **Cannon Rock** and some of the steepest cliffs in Guernsey.

Moulin Huet Bay lies below its charming valley and at its western end are the Dog and Lion Rocks. **Bon Port** is ahead, an inlet not to be reached by land, so sheer are the heights. Then comes **Saints Bay**, rather less severe-looking, with its delightful fishermen's harbour and Martello tower on the port side. The cliffs resume their stern expression as the boat sails towards **Icart**.

Its headland rears up with grandeur (as well it might, for it is the highest in the island) and people on the clifftop seem tiny. Savage-looking is **La Bette Bay**, with its dark-apertured Dog's Cave, but its more accessible neighbour, **Le Jaonnet**, seems slightly more amiable. It is a grand place to explore, though the approach is steep in places. The launch passes the cliffs of Mont Hubert, and ahead are the sands of **Petit Bôt**. A Martello tower and former water-mill stand above them and on the port side is St Clair Battery, on a low headland. On its far side is Portelet Bay, sandy and secluded, but difficult to reach.

The launch, at this point, may turn around and return to St Peter Port. Alternatively, depending on time and tide, she may continue to **Le Gouffre**, in which case some of the most spectacular of Guernsey's south coast scenery will be seen. **Les Sommeilleuses** cliffs are high and mighty, and the rocks below them wear a forbidding aspect. Ahead lies **La Pointe de la Moye** and in its lee is a deep water cove of much appeal. Here craft may lie safely, there are caverns to observe and green heights to survey, before the launch leaves this lovely scene and heads for harbour.

St Sampson's

From the Port of St Peter to that of St Sampson is a distance of only 3 miles (about 5km) and one could once make the journey by electric tram car. It was a pleasant ride, especially if you were on the upper deck or, better still, at the end of the 'toastrack' trailer, but the trams disappeared in 1934 and today buses replace them (*Bus Jl, J2, L1, L2*). But why not walk at least in one direction, using public transport in the other?

Such a stroll affords wonderful views of the Little Russel channel, the neighbouring islands and perhaps bird life in **Belle Grève Bay**, a large inlet wearing a fairer appearance at high tide than at low water. For part of the way there is an agreeable grass verge, with seats. On the landward side the prospect is utilitarian rather than picturesque and traffic is in variably busy. So walk and look seaward and in about half an hour you will be at St Sampson's Bridge, either via Grandes Maisons Road and New Road or by way of Bulwer Avenue, with its oil tanks and warehouses along part of the route. To use the second alternative turn right at Richmond Corner.

The stranger will look for **The Bridge** in vain; not so the islander, aware that it has long since disappeared. Until 1806 the northern part of Guernsey (known as Le Clos du Valle and incorporating Vale parish) was isolated from the rest of the island by a channel, Le Braye du Valle, extending from what is now St Sampson's harbour to Grand Havre, on the west coast. For years the threat of a French invasion was ever present and it was Lieutenant-General Sir John Doyle, the Lieutenant-Governor, who, believing Le Clos might afford a landing place and base for the enemy, ordered the reclamation of Le Braye, an undertaking which would then permit the garrison easier access to the north. The work was done and the former bridge between the large and small islands was absorbed in their union, yet the name endures for the shopping centre and western part of the harbour. In the centre of the Bridge a boundary stone marks the border between the parishes of St Sampson and the Vale.

The shops are numerous, well-stocked and popular. Offshoots of the Bridge have further shops: equally attractive are a few ancient houses. One of them, **Les Grandes Maisons** (some distance east of the shopping centre), stands in the road of that name, but it is only a shadow of its old self. Once it was the country house of the Le Marchant family, whose town residence was what is now the Royal Hotel. In Brock Road (off New Road) is a former inn, the Anchor and Hope, with a handsome arch. Further along this road are Les Maisons de Bas and de Haut (the Lower and Upper Houses), both of which are comparatively ancient.

At the upper extremity of Brock Road, just past Maison de Haut and the nearby Roman Catholic church of Our Lady, Star of the Sea, is **Delancey Park**. This green, informal place is used by sportsmen, children from the adjacent schools and visitors wishing to enjoy the view seaward. The children's playground on the slope is near the base of an obelisk destroyed by the Germans when they fortified this area. It commemorated Admiral Lord de Saumarez, a distinguished Guernseyman and a contemporary of Nelson. The plaques recalling his prowess are preserved at Castle Cornet.

On the northern slope of this little hill, overlooking the tennis courts, are the remains of a dolmen. It is a ruined structure, discovered in 1919, but of less interest than the megaliths further north. On the hill's eastern gradient is a bowling green. Hereabouts are German bunkers and a more comely gun battery of an earlier age, recalling the time when troops (including Russians in 1799) were in barracks on a site now covered by the schools. At that period troops fighting along with the English were not permitted in England; hence their presence here. The road passes by the school and, at the foot of the hill, turns left to the seafront, near the curiously-shaped Elim Pentecostal Church, built in 1982.

Returning to **St Sampson's harbour**, note its spaciousness and the excellence of its masonry. It is a great asset to the island, as it provides a port for the discharging of oil, coal, timber, cement and other bulk cargoes. It was built after the reclamation of the Braye, at a time when the export of stone was a thriving industry. Numerous quarries were worked in the northern parishes and it was sensible to have a harbour nearby. Until it was built, stone was loaded aboard vessels moored in creeks off the Braye, an operation only accomplished at low water.

With regard to Guernsey's industries, grapes and, later, tomatoes

PLACES OF INTEREST IN ST SAMPSON'S

Belle Grève Bay (*Bus J1, J2*)

Château des Marais, off Grand Bouet (*Bus J1, J2*) $^1/_4$-mile walk.

Grand Havre Bay
(*Bus H1, H2, K*)

Guernsey Candles
Petites Capelles
See craftsmen at work.
(*Bus H1, H2*).

Harbour
North and South Sides, also breakwater (*Bus J1, J2, K*).

Parish Church, off South Quay. Ancient building believed to stand near site where St Sampson landed in sixth century. Easter Sepulchre in St Magloire's chapel. Several medieval features, also Militia Colours and interesting memorials.
(*Bus J1, J2*).

Pottery and Glassworks
Oatlands, Braye Road.
See pottery-making and glass-blowing in unusual setting.
Refreshments. (*Bus L1, L2*).

were first raised under glass, most of it heated, during the nineteenth century. The coal and timber required were delivered at St Sampson's (where most of the vineries were sited), usually by the same ships that took away the granite. Until the enlargement of St Peter Port harbour in the 1850s, that port would have been quite incapable of handling such cargoes. St Sampson's only drawback is that it is tidal, but the materials handled are by no means perishable and sailings, in any event, can be regulated to suit most tidal conditions.

Today no granite is exported, chiefly because the nearby crushing plant was destroyed by the Germans during their Occupation. Although one of the quarries of A. & F. Manuelle, La Longue Hougue, resumed working after Liberation, in 1969 a major landslide occurred, resulting in many graves from the adjoining parish church yard falling into the quarry. Work was abandoned and today the vast aperture is used as a reservoir.

At the extremity of the harbour on the South Side is a finely-built breakwater, worth seeing for the workmanship displayed. Above it are a Martello tower and battery, standing on Mont Crevelt and occupying a strategic position overlooking the approaches to Guernsey and the entrance to the Braye du Valle in former times.

There is a touch of character about this northern port which many find attractive, even if it lacks the good looks of its more popular 'rival' in the south. Even when dry or devoid of ships the dressed stone should be examined, since nothing of the kind is produced nowadays. A further point of interest is the shipyard adjoining the Bridge, on the North Side. Here one may see quite large vessels (usually local), high and dry and undergoing overhaul or repairs.

This yard is reminiscent of the nineteenth century when shipbuilding was a major island industry. There were yards at St Peter Port, along Les Banques (the foreshore of Belle Grève) and at St Sampson's. The vessels were all sailers, with the exception of a solitary steamer, the *Commerce*. By no means were only local craft built, for many were engaged in the deep sea trade, and some were tea clippers. Nearly 200 were built between about 1820 and 1890, when sail began to decline and the yards were scarcely geared to construct steamers. They remained in business for some years, repairing vessels and the last shipyard, that of Peter Ogier, survived within living memory, where coal stores stand today on the South Side.

Close to this former shipyard a turning reveals what may well be Guernsey's most ancient place of worship, **St Sampson's Church**. It is dedicated to a saint who, it is believed, brought Christianity to the island in the sixth century and who is thought to have landed close by, building an oratory or chapel on the shore. Although the present building is much more recent, it may incorporate some of the fabric of something much older. Its style is rugged and there is no other Guernsey church quite like it, though rather similar are St Brelade's, Jersey, and a church at Mont St Michel, in Normandy.

Within the building the sense of age is equally strong. It has a special form of beauty, with the antique masonry furnishing a marked contrast with the Victorian glass and the mouldering Militia Colours in the chancel. The chapel of St Magloire, in the north aisle, has an Easter Sepulchre in the form of a shelf set at the angle of the north and east walls. Here, in pre-Reformation days, the Host was exposed

St Magloire's chapel in St Sampson's Church

at Easter-tide. Magloire, incidentally, was a kinsman of Sampson. On
the other side of the high altar is a window in the south aisle with

fourteenth-century tracery.

A memorial tablet on the south side of the chancel recalls Lieutenant Thomas Falla, killed in 1799 because 'of a wound from a solid cannon ball weighing 26lb, which had located itself between the two bones of one of his thighs'. This in itself was remarkable, but even more so was the fact that the surgeon only discovered the ball after Falla's death, 'to the surprise of the whole army', states the inscription, in French, with some exaggeration.

The church has a pre-Reformation chalice and other relics found in the tower in 1914 include a crucifix, censer and candlesticks, now displayed in St Magloire's chapel. The solitary bell in the tower was cast in 1759. A more modern relic is in the cemetery, a memorial commemorating the loss of the SS *Channel Queen* in 1898. It stands near that portion of the graveyard which collapsed in 1969. This area has been landscaped afresh and a stone cross stands on the massed grave containing the remains of those hurled into the quarry depths. The work carried out in this part of the cemetery is in admirable taste.

A WALK FROM DELANCEY TO LES CAPELLES

Although St Sampson's is chiefly an industrial region, the parish is not without its rural aspects, reminiscent of the days when commerce was less prevalent than it is now and when St Sampson's was nearly as pastoral as the Castel remains. A good example of its more gentle side is revealed in this walk near the western borders of the parish.

From the park cross Rue des Monts (on the west) and walk down Pointues Rocques, a lane whose name recalls a vanished prehistoric site. Cross the main road at St Clair (where a pre-Reformation chapel formerly stood) and opposite is Rue de Bas, a short hill descending to Duveaux Road. Opposite notice a large tomato vinery, one of several along the route. The word 'vinery' recalls the time when grapes were grown under glass, fruit now replaced by the ubiquitous 'Guernsey Tom', to use its trade name. A few Guernsey grapes are still grown and, to many, there are none more delicious.

Westward the way is bordered by fields, pleasant gardens and buildings old and new, with more trees than one might suppose in this part of the island. On the right is **Les Duveaux**, a fine old farm whose residence bears the date of 1805, Trafalgar year. Traces of an earlier

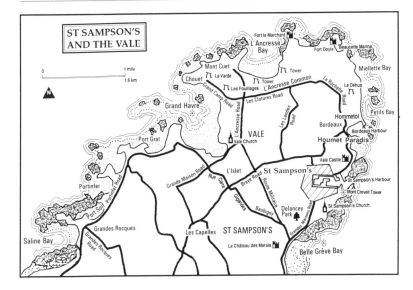

building exist and the property was originally vaster than it is today. Figs were once grown there under glass, but now the emphasis seems to be more on the rearing of Golden Guernsey goats (a recently developed breed both profitable and decorative) and in growing produce less exotic than figs. The goats are often accompanied by a donkey, the traditional animal of Guernsey, although not many are seen here.

At the end of the eighteenth century the farm figured briefly in a rather sensational phase in the island history. The Russian troops temporarily stationed at Delancey often roamed the countryside and on one occasion the farmer of Les Duveaux saw a soldier stealing his apples. The Russian, on being challenged, refused to desist and the enraged farmer shot him dead! The Ogier family have owned the property for generations and this aggressive representative, aghast at his crime, fled the island. He found sanctuary in the United States of America and, with other Guernseymen, established Guernsey County, in Ohio. The family cradle from Les Duveaux eventually crossed the Atlantic and is to be seen at Cambridge, Ohio.

Not far from this farm is another, **Baubigny**, alongside the road.

Opposite are livery stables and horses are to be seen there as well as along the neighbouring roads at times. Nearby, a disused quarry is now water-filled and ducks have adopted it, though a rather high wall makes observation difficult. Gone is Baubigny windmill, once employed in pumping water from the quarry.

A few hundred yards onward there is a turning left walking westward. Almost at once, again on the left, is a large grey building, **Baubigny Arsenal**, once the headquarters of the North Regiment of the Royal Guernsey Militia. It was here, in 1899, that the troops rebelled against their adjutant, a certain Captain Pym, whose harsh, unreasonable bearing was not to be endured. Court proceedings were instituted against the rebels, who were hailed as heroes after serving their prison sentences. Eventually Pym left the island and peace was restored.

Walk along Les Effards road, with its old buildings, new bungalows, colourful gardens and, inevitably, glasshouses. Trees line the way at times (chiefly Guernsey elms) and there is a prevailing air of the countryside. At the handsome house named 'Glen View' turn left, soon passing two interesting properties. On the one hand are more riding stables and on the other the impressive house and lands of Les Grandes Capelles.

Ahead is a crossroads and if one turns right along the main road one soon arrives at the settlement of **Les Capelles**, with its school and Methodist church. Turn right, down Les Petites Capelles road (through the traffic lights) to the Pony Inn. Grand Fort road follows and at Braeside crossroads (more traffic lights) there is an excellent pottery, glassworks and restaurant, in an unusual setting.

L' ISLET AND LE CHATEAU DES MARAIS

North of Braeside crossroads and inshore from Grand Havre is the modern village of **L'Islet** (*Bus L1, L2, H1, H2*), rich in places of worship, for there is St Mary's Church (Anglican), the Roman Catholic chapel of St Magloire and a strikingly modern Salvation Army building. (The Methodist church was closed recently.) About a quarter of a mile north is a collection of States (council) houses at Sandy Hook and in their midst is a megalithic tomb and cists. Local enquiry may be needed to locate them. In a cottage garden in nearby

Sandy Lane is a cist, covered by a massive stone and visible from the road. Some of the L'Islet buildings are of a pleasant appearance, but much of the district is industrial in character, with many glass houses and several disused quarries. Not far off is Vale Church and from here, as well as at L'Islet, buses to St Peter Port are available.

Before leaving St Sampson's parish, it is a good idea to visit **Le Château des Marais** (The Castle in the Marshes), locally styled the Ivy Castle, which lies about a quarter of a mile off the coast road from St Peter Port to St Sampson's. Here stands the Red Lion Hotel, a conspicuous feature, standing nearly opposite the former battery at La Hougue à la Perre (loosely translated as The Stony Hill) and here a road, Le Grand Bouet (the big, wooded, place) runs inland. Some distance on is Ivy Castle Lane (on the right-hand side) and this leads past a sprawling housing estate to the ancient ruined stronghold, standing on a mound above marshy terrain.

Its walls and moat have been restored recently and the main gate and eighteenth-century powder magazine are in good order. The castle is thought to date from the twelfth century and for a very long time it was disused. Yet in the Occupation the Germans thought fit to fortify it and one of their unlovely buildings survivod.

One may either return to the coast road on leaving the castle or regain St Peter Port by continuing along Le Grand Bouet and turning left at the traffic lights. This leads to Le Petit Bouet and St John's, whose 1838 church is worth seeing. From there to 'town' (as islanders invariably call St Peter Port) is not far to walk and if necessary buses are available at the Longstore.

The Vale Parish

On the North Side of St Sampson's harbour is the electricity generating station, serving the whole island. A short way beyond it, along the quay, will be noticed a massive stone chimney, rather like Victoria Tower in design. This stands in an area once occupied by the crushing mills, offices and stables of John Mowlem & Co, Ltd, one of the English contractors who quarried in Guernsey in the past. They abandoned Guernsey in 1929, but signs of their enterprise are not lacking and their business was continued by others for some years after.

Overlooking the northern approaches to the island and St Sampson's harbour is the **Vale Castle**, a fortress built on the edge of the former Clos du Valle, partly, perhaps, as a place of refuge for its people in time of war and also as a defence work on a commanding site. However, it is a building with little history, until 1799, when Russian troops were quartered there, as well as in other parts of the island. At the time it was illegal to billet foreign soldiers in England and the men, fighting alongside the English troops in the Netherlands, were therefore sent to Guernsey to rest. They were not very popular and the guns of Castle Cornet were trained on them as they sailed away, to ensure that they did not return!

The coast road northward skirts Vale Castle hill, but it is preferable to use the footpath on its seaward side. Half a mile onward is **Bordeaux** harbour, an engaging little fishing haven, full of moored boats, with a fine sandy beach as its neighbour. There is a stone pier and a slipway, too, both covered at high tide. Seats and a refreshment place encourage one to pause and gaze at a very attractive scene, especially when the tide is full. Herm is quite near.

There is a path around the inlet, running past a quarry formerly used as a rubbish disposal site. When this valuable land has been reclaimed then the region will be even more agreeable than it is. Meanwhile, on the foreshore by St Sampson's oil tanks, much spoil and rubbish are gradually are being used to fill a space which, ultimately, will provide the island with some additional and much needed land.

The houses of Bordeaux are, for the most part, as good to see as the bay. Especially fine is Maison Bordeaux, a few yards inland from the bay's centre and of great antiquity. More modern, and perhaps more agreeable, is the stone house of Les Rocques Barrées (The Barred Rocks), set in gardens and verdant fields by the roadside. Above them is the Vale windmill, its original form spoilt by German additions, though it is still a landmark.

At the northern extremity of the inlet is a small islet, Hommet, easily reached and the place in which to rest and watch. Its

Vale Castle, Bordeaux

neighbour, close by, is bigger and is one of a group of fascinating 'high tide islets', known as **Les Houmets**. One may approach them dryshod at low water, or thereabouts, but keep an eye on the tide and if, by any chance, you are marooned on one of them, do not attempt to wade or swim back, since the tide between the islets and the shore is dangerous. This warning, however, rarely applies to the first of them, for Houmet Benest is surrounded for only a brief period.

In the Napoleonic Wars a gun battery was built there, so as to protect Bordeaux from the north. Dense vegetation masks its precise whereabouts today, but a German gun position near the older one is quite visible. Les Houmets abound in wild flowers and plants and the degree of solitude they offer is out of all proportion to their size and their proximity to a very much busier environment.

The best of the trio is Houmet Paradis, the central islet, and the largest. Traces of fields as well as quarrying can be seen, despite the profusion of gorse, bracken and much else. The ruins of a quarrymen's hut are visible and so are the scars left by the Germans,

Bordeaux Harbour

Le Déhus dolmen

for both the northern and southern ends of this *'houmet'* have been mutilated. Like Houmet Benest, it was a fortified position in World War II. Houmet Paradis figures in Victor Hugo's romance, *The Toilers of the Sea*, although he makes it a promontory rather than an islet. 'Paradis' is derived from a nearby estate bearing this name, lying less than half a mile away and facing a disused quarry, now a beautiful bird sanctuary.

Just north of Houmet Paradis is Hommetol, less visited (although none of Les Houmets is ever overcrowded), smaller and perhaps wilder than its fellows, since it is set in a perfect wilderness of rocks. It is a weird place over which the wind moans, gulls cry and the sound of the sea is always heard. At low water its natural causeway can be approached via the beach, without too great a scramble.

Continuing northward, the alternative route from Houmet Paradis is to take the road running west (Le Parc Lane) and then turn right. This way passes **Le Déhus dolmen**, one of the island's finest and worth a visit. The rude carving of a face has been cut in one of the

L'Ancresse Bay

capstones and there are side chambers to examine. The dolmen's mound was restored in the 1930s. Prior to this its ancient stones were visible to the passer-by.

Walking along this lane in a northerly direction there is a turning right (Miellette Lane), which eventually runs down to the shore opposite Hommetol. Having visited it there is the choice of a beach scramble northwards, towards the Beaucette yacht marina (whose masts are visible), or a retracing of Miellette Lane until it bears right. This goes past the Paradis house and its lovely old quarry.

The road, still northwards, passes a still more ancient house, St Magloire, now used as a store. The saint is said to have built a chapel hereabouts. Just a few hundred yards onward is the yacht marina, overlooked by a restaurant and with facilities for yachtsmen. This was the first of Guernsey's marinas and was created out of a disused quarry. A thin barrier of rock separated this from the sea, and, when it was breached, its maritime entrance was almost ready-made.

L'Ancresse (*Bus J1, J2, K, L1, L2*) is Guernsey's north-eastern

❋ extremity, where **Fort Doyle** stands. Offshore is the Platte Fougère lighthouse, built in 1909 and operated automatically. Its appearance is unlovely, but its boon to the mariner is undoubted. More than one ship has foundered on this reef before the installation of the lighthouse and fog signal, which are powered by a cable running from Fort Doyle.

Fort Doyle was one of the many coastal defences built by Sir John Doyle in the eighteenth century and, like its fellows, it was given a new lease of life in this century, thanks to the Germans. Old fortifications were situated on commanding sites and the invaders were quick to appreciate this and used them accordingly. Unhappily, the adaptations were of concrete and the aged buildings often lost some of their appeal.

❋ The eastern end of L'Ancresse Common, is one of Guernsey's greatest attractions. Here one may enjoy golf, walks, lazing in the sun, watching the sea, ships, aircraft, birds or the sky. Goats and cattle graze there, unconcerned by man's activities. There is room for all in this spacious green region of the island.

❋ Notice L'Ancresse's numerous coastal defences, since its open bay was so vulnerable to attack. A string of so-called Martello towers flank the shore. In fact, they were built before the true Martello was thought of, but the name is commonly used and is convenient. Their weathered stone is fine to see and it is a pity that they are somewhat neglected, especially as they are scheduled ancient monuments. One was destroyed by the Germans, who made use of the remainder.

❋ **Fort le Marchant** stands on Guernsey's most northern promontory, east of the bay. It should be visited. On the west is the less interesting Fort Pembroke and between them were several batteries, some of which survive. A German anti-tank wall lines the bay, although the shores of the more rocky Fontenelle Bay is not so protected. The inlet lies between Forts Doyle and le Marchant and is little visited. A coastal path skirts it and leads to Fort le Marchant.

L'Ancresse beach is very popular; its sands are broad, one may dive from its rocks, its pools are worth inspecting and the sea is pellucid. The broad inlet has room for all, but most people are to be found at Pembroke, at the western end. At either extremity are places of refreshment, where chairs, floats and souvenirs are obtainable.

PLACES OF INTEREST
IN VALE AND L'ANCRESSE

L'Ancresse Common
Golf, good walking country, prehistoric remains (especially Les Fouillages burial chamber), old and new fortifications. Refreshments, fine bay nearby. (*Bus J1, J2, L1, L2, K*).

Beaucette Marina
Guernsey's first, set in former quarry near Fort Doyle. (*Buses J1 and J2 pass near marina*).

Bordeaux
Fishing haven and attractive beach. (*Bus J1, J2, K*).

Le Déhus Dolmen
Guernsey's finest Megalithic burial chamber, side chambers may be examined. Restored in 1930s.

Parish Church
One of most ancient on the island. Prehistoric tombstone near entrance. Fine belfry. Interesting churchyard. (*Bus L1, L2, K*).

Vale Castle
Ruin, but ramparts worth seeing, if only for view. (*Bus J1, J2*).

Buses are frequent and those running to Pembroke discharge at the bay itself. Those serving the eastern end stop a short distance from the beach.

Before leaving L'Ancresse walk around Le Chouet headland, starting from Pembroke Bay Hotel. A path runs to the fort and turns left to **Baie de la Jaonneuse**, a favourite spot with those seeking relative seclusion. It then continues westward. In the quarry lies a great German tower, which formerly stood on the summit. The coastal path runs past another Martello tower before returning to the common.

Immediately above is a low hill and on its summit is **La Varde** **dolmen**, rather inconspicuous, but worthy of a visit. The Germans heavily fortified this height, but they spared this ancient burial place. From here one looks down on the golf club house and a great expanse of sea. On a clear day Les Casquets lighthouse and Alderney are visible.

Below La Varde are other Neolithic burial chambers, chief of which is **Les Fouillages**, standing beside a green on the links. It was discovered accidentally in 1977 and excavated during 1978-81. The result was a major archaeological find, arousing world-wide attention. The director of the 'dig', Dr Ian Kinnes, Assistant Keeper in the Department of Prehistoric and Romano-British Antiquities at the British Museum, declared the monument to be 7,000 years old and unique in western Europe. The finds were of great importance and the entire undertaking, sponsored by the States of Guernsey Ancient Monuments Committee, was watched by many spectators and widely reported.

A few yards away is the less impressive tomb of La Platte Mare and on the golf course, eastward, are traces of kindred monuments. This part of Guernsey was rich in such remains and, while many have been destroyed, a number survive, especially in the north. They include La Rocque qui Sonne, to be seen in the Vale School playground, near the Vale Mill.

 One of Guernsey's largest bays, **Grand Havre**, lies west of L'Ancresse. When the tide fills it, the inlet looks striking, while at low water, what a paradise it is for the marine prowler! It is one of the most interesting bays, since there are two admirable fishing harbours to see, at Les Amarreurs on the east and Rousse opposite, on the west, near which a Martello and battery stand guard. At the so-called 'Ladies Bay' is an expanse of sand extending from Le Chouet to Les Amarreurs. There is more sand as the bay continues westward and many boats lie at offshore moorings, adding interest to the scene.

Here, prior to 1806, the channel of the Braye du Valle entered the sea, although at low tide it was dry. A vestige of the Braye survives nearly opposite Vale Church. It is now a nature reserve and a good place in which to observe bird life.

The **Vale Church** is not to be missed, for it is one of Guernsey's most ancient places of worship and, for centuries, it had as its neighbour Vale Priory. Unhappily, this has been demolished and the rectory occupies part of its site, but the ancient church stands on its mound as it has done for perhaps a thousand years. Enter it, and savour the aura of age it enjoys. Observe its Norman aspects, notice the strange sanctuary arch, experience the peace of the Chapel of the Holy Angels. In the tower is the ringing chamber and outside is an early monument, possibly a menhir 'Christianised' with a cross. It was unearthed in the churchyard in 1949.

Buses pass the church, but, before leaving it, examine the lychgate. Its inscription, in French, reveals that it was blessed by the Archbishop of Canterbury, Dr Michael Ramsey, when he visited Guernsey in 1973, the first archbishop to do so. The ride back to St Peter Port ends the long but worthwhile exploration of northern Guernsey. Some of its lanes should be seen, but leave this for another day.

A Note On Cliff Walks

Primarily, these walks are designed for those without their own transport, although it may well be possible to leave cars at a convenient spot, enjoy the walk and return to the vehicle. It is better to use buses, for one may travel to a starting place, walk and take another bus at the end of the stroll. Bus stops are so marked on road surfaces and all buses return to the St Peter Port terminus. To appreciate the cliffs fully, walking is essential, although again buses may be used.

Obviously, visitors must use their own initiative to some extent and the walks to be described can be adjusted to taste. Invaluable are Perry's Guide Maps to the Bailiwick. On the cliffs, invariably keep to the paths and avoid, at all costs, climbing up or down where no path exists. However inviting and easy it may seem to 'explore', respect these glorious but sometimes forbidding heights and follow the accepted way only. By the same token, do not use fields or other private property as short cuts. Take care with matches and discarded cigarettes, for while it is all too easy to start a cliff fire it is much more difficult to extinguish it. To contaminate cliffs and other open spaces with litter is something no decent-minded person would dream of doing. Public conveniences are to be found at most bays and at some viewpoints.

At the time of writing, the state of cliff and coastal paths is good on all the islands, but there can be no guarantee that this will always be so. The author and publishers, therefore, cannot accept any responsibility in the event of readers encountering trouble. At all times take care on the cliffs and shores of the islands.

St Martin's and The Forest

(*Bus B, C1, C2, and Petit Bôt minibus*)
St Martin's Church (*Bus A & B*) is set in beautiful surroundings, has an ornate south porch and a well designed tower. Within, is a pulpit of 1655, some interesting memorials, modern windows of merit and the three bells date from 1736. Below the building is the settlement of La Bellieuse, abounding in gracious old houses set in beautiful gardens. What an oasis is this after the tumult of the main roads so close by! The energetic can walk from here via lanes to St Peter Port, a distance of about 2 miles.

The spire of the parish church can be seen from Grande Rue, where most of the shops are situated. A little distance downhill stands a remarkable antiquity, standing at the churchyard's gate: it is 'La Grand' Mère du Chimquière' (The Great Mother of the Cemetery), a statue menhir of exceeding rarity. Clearly prehistoric, it was almost certainly an idol and the sculpting of tough Guernsey granite into the semblance of a female figure is amazing. There are signs of an attempt to cut it in two, but the stone's resistance foiled the vandal who, no doubt, felt indignant at the respect paid to the figure as late as the last century. Even today people sometimes place coins on her head 'for luck', and on occasion a floral garland is found around her neck. There are times when wedding groups pose beside La Grand' Mère, whose presence in the photograph must be baffling to the uninitiated!

No visit to St Martin's should omit **Sausmarez Manor** from its itinerary. On certain days it is open to the public and its setting alone is well worth viewing. The present house dates from Queen Anne's reign and is, perhaps, Guernsey's finest residence. The entrance gates bear the arms and supporters of the island's most ancient family, whose heirlooms are among the exhibits shown. A house stood on the site in the thirteenth century and a fragment of it survives. The estate has been in this family's hands for several generations and some of its sons have added materially to the history of the island and the nation. Beside the gates is the court house of Fief de Sausmarez (whose Seigneur resides at the manor) and at Les

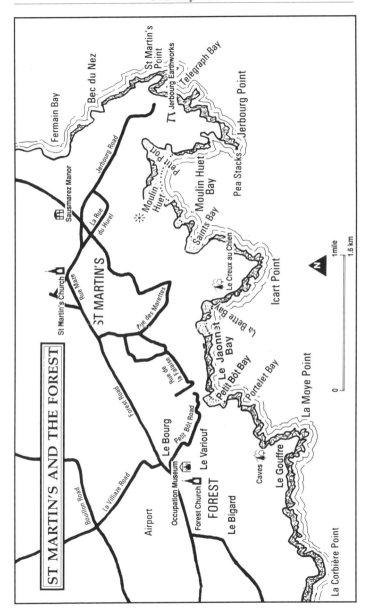

ST MARTIN'S AND THE FOREST

Camps du Moulin, close to the parish war memorial, is the tower of the manorial windmill. It stands on the road to Le Vallon, a former house of the Carey family.

From the manor gates walk left for a few yards and then take the turning right, which follows Le Varclin valley. On reaching Calais Lane look out for the stone sign pointing to the cliff path running down to Fermain Bay.

Fermain Bay itself is one of the most popular and attractive of Guernsey's bays and may be approached several ways, all of which are agreeable. Perhaps the best of all is to go there by launch from St Peter Port. The journey is all too brief, for the distance is about a couple of miles (4km) with a view of the imposing Castle Cornet from sea level and then the cliffs below Fort George are seen at close quarters. This approach to Fermain, preferably on a full tide, is unforgettable, for cliffsides and valley are richly wooded, and the heights, although lofty enough, have a gentle touch, a quality missing from their sterner neighbours further off. One lands on the beach by means of a mobile stage and the joy of Fermain is at your feet.

Another route, and one more strenuous, is from La Vallette over the cliffs, a walk full of beauty, meandering through copses, with many a glimpse of the gleaming sea and of the aged walls of Fort George, with seats and steps to aid the pedestrian, who reaches Fermain after about l.75 miles (3km) via the moorings (actually a stone landing place used today more by swimmers and divers than by fishermen, although several craft are moored nearby). Paths are well signposted by means of granite pillars, with directions inscribed thereon.

An alternative way to Fermain is by road and this is less attractive, though the walk through Fort George is interesting and the military cemetery, with its British soldiers' graves, is well worth seeing. Just beyond it the road turns left, through Village de Putron, then runs steeply down to Le Becquet, a headland overlooking the bay, with a curious white 'Pepper Pot' seamark, once a sentry box. Paths down to Fermain are simple to follow.

Yet one more road route available is to proceed along the Fort Road (either via Hauteville and George Road or La Charroterie and Colborne Road) until Fermain Hotel is reached. It lies a short distance

PLACES OF INTEREST IN ST MARTIN'S

Jerbourg
Traces of Iron Age fort near Doyle monument. German defences. Fine cliffs. Refreshments. (*Bus A1*).

Parish Church
Statue menhir at entrance. Fine architecture (especially porch), good modern glass, ancient pulpit. Building set in beautiful surroundings. (*Bus A2, B*).

Sausmarez Manor
Sausmarez Road.

Guernsey's only 'stately home' open to public. Elegant house in fine grounds. Feudal court-house beside heraldic gates. Guided tours.
(*Bus A and B*).

Note
Petit Port, Moulin Huet and Saints are all most attractive bays, though they involve walking from bus stops or car parks.
(Bus B).

beyond the Morley Youth Hostel. At the hotel, turn left down Fermain Lane and enjoy the steep, beautiful, descent to the bay. En route are hotels set in highly attractive grounds, where refreshments are available, as they are near the Martello tower beside the ancient rampart above the beach. One may not drive to the bay, but parking is permitted in Rue de Putron and Becquet Road, off the Fort Road, and from this one walks down to the Pepper Pot and so to the beach.

The bay can also be reached by an excellent cliff path from Jerbourg, another outstanding place to be visited. Thus Fermain can be approached by a variety of attractive routes, none of which exhausts its users. Fermain valley is enlivened by a stream, serving as the boundary between St Peter Port and St Martin's parishes. It runs between massive stone walls on its way to the sea, bastions to thwart the invader, like the batteries overlooking the bay.

Swimming is best at high water, when there are fewer pebbles to negotiate, although then there will be no sand. It is a popular place, yet there is ample room for all. Floats are available and these, with the coming and going of yachts, launches and other craft, present a lively spectacle. On the right of the bay, reached by cliff path, is **Le**

The Great Mother of the Cemetery, St Martin's

St Martin's Church

Grand Creux, a deep cave worth viewing and more impressive than the cavern on the left of the beach.

For the energetic, the cliff path from Fermain to Jerbourg presents no problems. The distance is short, the surface good, and the view, as always, is splendid. Seats are available and there are places to visit on the way. From Fermain the path climbs up to the cliff-top settlement of Calais, but before the buildings are reached bear left (stone guide marks point the way) and walk south before descending the valley to **Bec du Nez**. This is a good, out of the way, sort of place, with its fishing haven, boats, and opportunities for bathing when the tide is not too low. On the slopes are pine copses and, as ever on the Guernsey cliffs, gorse adds a touch of gold to the prospect.

Bec du Nez, like its fellows on the east coast, is at its best in the morning. A little further south is the ambitiously named Pine Forest, in reality but a handful of trees and, while it has its merits, the beach below is better. This is the so-called **Marble Bay**, whose proper name is Pied du Mur (Foot of the Wall), recalling the bygone Jerbourg Castle on the nearby promontory.

The quartz visible on the beach has a marble-like appearance, hence the name. From this place a path at a low level leads southwards to St Martin's Point, or another, uphill, to Jerbourg. It is preferable to continue to the Point, from which Jerbourg may be reached. Guernsey's cliffs are glorious, but they can only be enjoyed to the full by walkers, who must expect a measure of effort in their explorations. Others can drive (or walk a little way) to headlands and enjoy the views.

The headland of **St Martin's Point** is not a bold one, for it slopes gently from 300ft down to sea level. Below it, is the inlet of Vaux Bêtes (Valley of Beasts, although it is not, in fact, overrun by animals), but it is commonly called **Telegraph Bay**, because of the cable which used to run from here to Jersey. A small, automatically-operated lighthouse and fog signal stand on a low headland, near which is an old battery — the whole is a scene of beauty. It is secluded and often fishermen are the only signs of humanity there. The rather plain-looking lighthouse and concrete bridge leading there do not impair the scene; perhaps they enhance it.

The climb up the slope to **Jerbourg** (*Bus A*) should be taken

Cliff path from Fermain Bay to Bec du Nez and Marble Bay

Sausmarez Manor

leisurely. At the top refreshments are available. The seaward view is very wide and wonderful, with Jersey and the other islands visible, together with the French coast on a clear day. A good path runs southward past bungalows to Jerbourg Point, overlooking the finest chain of rocks in the Channel Islands.

They are the **Peastacks** (Les Tas de Pois d'Amont), seen to better advantage from a boat, when their height and grandeur can be fully appreciated. One of them, viewed from a certain angle, resembles the figure of a man and it is known as 'Le Petit Bon Homme d'Andrilot' (The Good Little Man named Andrew) and it was once an object of veneration. Passing fishermen were in the habit of doffing their caps and lowering their topsails out of respect for this granite object which, at close quarters, seems to be more of a giant than a good little man.

Unhappily, German defences dominate both Jerbourg Point and other sites in this glorious region and it is better to take a look at the much older gun battery above Le Havre des Moies, in the shadow of the Peastacks. A path near the battery leads down to sea level and for the really agile it is quite possible to scramble from one great rock to another, finishing at the 100ft Great Peastack itself, whose bulk, from a distance, resembles a lion's head. The sea here is deep and the diver will have the time of his life on this enormous stack. To swim from shore to this rock is easy and, for the enthusiast, an experience not soon forgotten. Obviously, tide and weather conditions must be studied beforehand. One German battery near the Peastacks (with a seat on the roof) is kept swept out, includes a bench seat and provides shelter from the rain as well as a reminder of the war.

There is an excellent path around the Jerbourg headland, on the west side of which lie the sands of Petit Port. There is a wonderful vista of sea, cliffs, rocks, flowers and sky, with the incessant cry of the birds from the Peastacks. The track passes above the **Cannon Rock**, a huge pillar (easily reached and climbed, and approached either by path or from the sands) and best seen from the bay. Above, on the headland, are traces of an Iron Age monument, better reached from the end of the path, near the bus route.

Here, on a mound, a monument confronts you. It commemorates a great Guernsey Lieutenant-Governor, Sir John Doyle, but this is not the original memorial; the Germans destroyed that lest it should serve as a landmark for their vast fortifications in this region. The first pillar was taller and hollow and steps led to the summit, from which a grand view rewarded the climber. The present obelisk still makes a good place from which to survey the scene, with the aid of a 'view finder', which tells you what you are observing. There is a car park, bus stop and place of refreshment nearby.

To some, there is one great disadvantage about **Petit Port** (*Bus B*): the long flight of steps leading to it. Going down is simple, but the ascent can be exhausting. The reward, of course, is the magnificent expanse of sand at low tide, the majesty of the steep cliffs, the shelter and peace of this beauty spot and the excellent bathing it offers. A possible, though dubious, alternative to the climb is to go to nearby Moulin Huet Bay and, at low water (preferably a low spring tide) walk along a sandy fringe of bay to Petit Port. Such a journey may well entail wet feet, will give you very little time to spend at Petit Port and, on the whole, has little to recommend it, save the pleasure of the scramble itself. To enjoy Petit Port, the steps must be used (or perhaps a steep path just west of them, entailing just as much effort), but once down, the caves invite exploration, especially one with a *creux* (an aperture in the roof) and the broad sands afford opportunities for fun and games. At times there is surf to add to the joys of this remarkable, if somewhat unattainable, south coast jewel.

For most, **Moulin Huet Bay** (*Bus B*) is to be preferred to its more sandy neighbour. Its beauty is unrivalled, it has achieved fame in verse and painting, and its various approaches are glorious. One of them is a walk over the cliffs from Petit Port, which is as enjoyable as the similar journey from Saints Bay, either of which covers a bare half mile. Most, however, go to Moulin Huet by road, entailing a little walking either from the bus stop or valley car park. The attractive and justly famous water lane, via the hamlet of La Ville Amphrey is the traditional approach.

On the way from the bus stop notice the remains of the de Sausmarez windmill on the left of the road, which soon descends to the wishing well at the head of the water lane. From here a rather damp path bears the stream company as it descends to the valley. A car park is near and from it an easy descent takes one to the bay,

Tower, Fermain Bay

Hotel in the Fermain Valley

above which is a place of refreshment. Equally attractive is the approach from La Fosse (where there is a bus stop), by way of a wooded valley road so lovely that to traverse it by car seems to be an affront. Trees, streams, comely buildings and flower-decked slopes grace the approaches to Moulin Huet, whose name recalls the water mill which once stood in the hamlet above the bay.

At low water there is some sand and many, having descended the steps, make for the far end of the beach; but as this can only be reached when the tide permits, the return may be difficult. At other times there is swimming to be enjoyed in rock gullies, though at high water accommodation is a little cramped. It is, all in all, a very lovely place, with its massive Cradle Rock in the centre and, away to the west, the Dog and Lion Rocks, best seen from the cliffs towards Saints Bay.

Above Moulin Huet are the wooded grounds of **Le Vallon**, a fine house, once a seat of the Carey family. It can be approached from the Jerbourg road and the walk to Le Vallon from the main road is enjoyable, although the house itself is not open to view. A nearby lane will take you to the cliff-top hamlet of Le Mont Durand and from there is easy access to the Jerbourg road bus stops or car park. This road is busy and narrow, which is rather a pity, since, on either side, there is so much to see.

Precisely how **Saints Bay** (*Bus B*) received its name is by no means clear, although some say it is so called because of two rocks, shaped like saints (!) on the left of the bay. The bus takes one to the top of the valley road and there is rather limited parking on the way down. It is pleasant to wander to the beach by this country lane, but en route make a detour by using the right-hand turning, with a stream to ford first. This narrow road passes a Martello tower and leads to a very attractive fishermen's harbour.

Here is a handsome granite pillar, commemorating a Seigneur of Blanchelande, whose fief, or manor, stood on high ground close by and is largely occupied by Blanchelande College. He helped to pay for the haven's construction in the last century.

The Germans fortified this area and callously pitched the obelisk onto the beach. Years after the Occupation it was hauled back and reinstated. The bathing, at high tide, is good and the presence of boats and their gear, as well as the slipway and cavern-like boat house, are as enjoyable as the spot itself. Rather too many motorists are prone to use it, though, for parking is extremely limited. Close to Saints Bay proper is a refreshment place.

The magnificent headland of **Icart** (*Bus B*) separates two broad inlets, with Moulin Huet on one side and Petit Bôt on the other. A bus will take you to within half a mile of the point, near which is a car park and place of refreshment. The walker is advised to leave the bus at the top of Saints Hill and instead of descending it proceed inland, turn left and walk along the interesting Icart Road. Alternatively, stay in the bus until the next stop after Saints, and then start walking.

After one or two interesting farmhouses, the view begins to emerge and it is a good plan to leave the road a few hundred yards from the bus stop, turn left and join the cliff path running south. A wide prospect reveals Saints, Moulin Huet cliffs, Petit Port and the Jerbourg promontory. At Icart Point the cliff slopes down to La Petite Coupée, a crumbling isthmus leading to a rock mass, now in so

Moulin Huet

dangerous a state that it is called off. From the Point another wide view lies westward, embracing Petit Bôt, the great cliffs on either side of it, and rugged Pointe de la Moye in the distance.

It is an invigorating cliff journey from Icart to **Petit Bôt Bay** (*Bus C1, C2, & Mini*), covering some 2 miles (about 4km) and passing above the beautiful cove of Le Jaonnet, reached by a good path and steps. At low tide one may walk from its sands to those of La Bette, in which is the yawning Dog's Cave, of noble proportions. These little bays are visited by only a few, which makes them the more enjoyable, even though access may be rather laborious.

The cliff path continues westward, with prospects to savour. Ultimately it descends to the main valley road from La Villette and Petit Bôt is reached. The motorist can drive down this really lovely valley via La Villette (approached from the Forest Road) or from another, equally good, from Le Bourg, near the Forest Church. A minibus also runs to and from the bay from Le Bourg.

At Petit Bôt there is a refreshment house, a Martello tower and the

Saints Bay

meagre remains of two watermills. Little is left of the upper mill (destroyed by the Germans), save its wheel, but the lower mill-house survives as a restaurant. Streams flow down the valleys and, just above the bay, the water is pumped up again, leaving only a trickle to flow over the beach, which forms the boundary between St Martin's and the Forest parishes.

Beyond the tower is the cliff path and, using it, the walker soon reaches a left-hand turn. Follow it and pause at St Clair Battery, overlooking both Petit Bôt and **Portelet Bay**, the latter being an agreeable little cove, sandy and quieter than its larger neighbour. It is reached by taking another path close to the start of that running to the battery and the slight effort required will not be wasted; at high tide access to the beach is impossible.

Portelet visited, resume the main cliff path and after an inland turn see the majestic headland of **La Moye** and its highly attractive fishing harbour beside and below it. A way down reveals a pair of timber 'rails' by which, aided by a windlass, boats were hauled up the cliff for the winter. Craft are moored in this deep water inlet and at a low spring tide it is possible to explore the nearby Fontenelle caves, below the heights of Les Sommeilleuses. Moye Point is easily climbed and its rugged grandeur is memorable.

The cliff path widens as it approaches **Le Gouffre**, a savage gulf at the end of a thickly wooded ravine. At its head is a handful of buildings, including a restaurant. The path continues behind it, running westward, and from here to Pleinmont Point the popular sandy bays are left behind and a wild, splendid coastline is the reward of the walker. In this region, as elsewhere, those who prefer to see the cliffs without effort may do so from the car parks to be found at practically every headland and reached from the main roads, along which buses run.

Next is the cliffside hamlet of **Le Bigard**, highly attractive with its ancient houses and sense of seclusion. The path continues along the cliff edge and leads to **La Corbière Point**, one of the finest in the island. Its rock strata are of an unusual type, the views are extensive, seats allow visitors to enjoy them in comfort. Below, reached by a good path, is **Havre de Bon Repos** (Haven of Good Rest), an ironical name, for any ships 'resting' there would surely lie shattered — so rocky is this savage place. Years ago somebody took the trouble to construct a small swimming pool in the rocks, bearing the romantic name of 'Venus's Pool'. Care should be taken in approaching the bay, since rock falls may be encountered.

The trail goes up to **Prévôté Tower**, a stout German building replacing an older watch-house. Some of the cliff land here is owned by the National Trust of Guernsey, which also has property at Jerbourg, Pleinmont and on the west coast. The way westward is clear and soon it passes Guernsey's biggest cave, Le Creux Mahié. One can approach it by a track, but it is scarcely worth the effort, for it is dark, dirty and dangerous, due to possible rock falls. Far preferable is the view from the clifftop.

Ahead the headland of **Les Tielles** beckons. It is a beauty-spot easily reached by car or bus. In spring it is a paradise of wild flowers and is always attractive. German work replaces a ruined watch-house, but a little way below its site is a well-preserved eighteenth-century battery, paved and flower-decked. Les Tielles car park is protected by a low wall, since the cliffs here are high and sheer. At about this point the parishes of the Forest and St Peter-in-the-Wood meet. The bus route is near and the visitor may well pass a while in and around the Forest Church.

Petit Bôt bay

Forest

Le Bourg is a collection of dwellings whose neighbour, La Villiaze Airport (built in 1939), is but an infant compared with the antiquity of the village. At the top of the Petit Bôt valley road is **Le Péron du Roi** (King's Mounting Block), a short menhir of untold age. It once served horsemen who moved in procession around the island to visit ceremonially sections of the King's Highway, among other tasks, although despite its name, the king did not use the mounting block. This ceremony was called *La Chevauchée*. Several Guernsey churches stand beside prehistoric monuments, strongly suggesting that early missionaries strove to offset the supposed influence of pagan objects (menhirs and megaliths chiefly) by building Christian places of worship on or near their sites. The **Forest Church** (*Bus C1, C2*) is a typical example.

It is Guernsey's smallest parish church and, like the others (Torteval excepted), it must be approaching its millennium. (Precise dates of their building are lacking, but almost certainly they evolved from chapels to their present proportions.) Perhaps its eastern end is the most ancient part and here one finds a well-preserved piscina, where the priest rinsed his hands at Mass. In the diminutive tower are four bells, and the clock (so often anxiously consulted by those hurrying to the airport) is a memorial of Queen Victoria's Diamond Jubilee. During the Occupation this was the only church that was closed as it was too near to the airport for safety.

Very near the church and easily found (it is well signposted) is the **German Occupation Museum**, well worth seeing. It is housed in a cottage opposite a farmhouse and, though relatively small, it is full of most valuable and sometimes poignant reminders of one of the most important chapters in Guernsey history. Running downhill in a south-easterly direction is an attractive lane. If followed to its extremity it will turn into Petit Bôt Valley, by the Manor Hotel. Alternatively, it is rewarding at this point, to turn right, rather than left, and climb up to **Le Variouf**, one of the island's most enchanting hamlets. Farms, cottages, gardens — all are lovely and Le Variouf should be seen, whether one ultimately descends to Petit Bôt or continues past the

PLACES OF INTEREST IN FOREST

German Occupation Museum
near church.
Excellent display of varied relics,
military and domestic.
(*Bus C1, C2*).

Le Gouffre
Savage gulf, near La Moye
Point. Restaurant. About $1/_2$ mile
from nearest bus stop.
(*Bus C1, C2*).

Gouffre Picture Gallery
opposite restaurant.
Parking.

Parish Church
Smallest in Guernsey but worth
visiting.
(*Bus C1, C2*).

Petit Bôt
Charming bay and equally
attractive approach either from
La Villette or Le Bourg. Former
paper mill now a restaurant.
Parking.
(*Bus M, C1, C2*, last two involve
walking down valley.)

hamlet to Les Fontenelles and its neighbour, Le Gouffre.

Another secluded and engaging approach to Petit Bôt is the water lane running off the Forest road just east of Le Chêne Hotel, close to the traffic lights. The way is for walkers only and it is both easy and full of attractions. Eventually the lane joins the valley road running down from La Villette and one crosses a shallow ford at its end. The bay lies a short distance away on the right.

To return to St Martin's 'village' from Le Bourg one may take the Forest Road, rather a dull and, certainly, a busy highway, though not a very long one. The walker would do better to walk to La Chêne traffic lights and then turn left. The road proceeds in somewhat winding fashion and reaches Rue des Agneaux (Sheep Road), proceeding east. This becomes Le Chemin du Roi (the old King's Highway) and it runs parallel with the Forest Road. It passes the Haut Nez water tower, standing on Guernsey's highest point: 342ft (104m) above sea level. Some fine old houses stand at Les Mouilpieds, near which the road joins a secondary road and is united with the Forest Road at Les Cornus. From this point to St Martin's shopping centre is not more than half a mile.

Portelet Bay, Forest

Torteval and St Peter-in-the-Wood

TORTEVAL (*BUS C1 & C2*)

To many, these south-western parts of Guernsey are some of its best, since the heavy hand of development has fallen more lightly here than elsewhere. The cliffs are majestic, the low-lying shores have a strong appeal and the interior reveals a countryside not much different from what it was a century ago. Here, as in other parts of the island, it is the walker who sees most, although the motorist (or bus passenger) can still enjoy a great deal by a judicious mixture of riding and walking.

 From Les Tielles to Pleinmont Point runs a magnificent stretch of cliffland and if it can be seen in late spring or early summer it will then be at its loveliest, since flowers, trees, grass and other vegetation wear a dress not to be matched later in the year. After a few hundred yards of westward walking, look back and notice the fine natural arch below Les Tielles. Ahead is **Mont Hèrault watchhouse**, conspicuous, yet, at close quarters, rather insignificant, since it is but a sturdy cottage. Its situation lends it grandeur, a quality disregarded by the vandal, whose attentions have not left this antiquity unscathed.

 A track down the cliff leads to the small inlet of **Belle Elizabeth**, where there is a cave. The name, legend declares, is derived from that of a lovely girl who plunged to her death after her parents had forbidden her to marry her lover. A rock offshore is said to be the petrified maiden! Close by is Long Avalleur (Great Slope), a fine section of cliff like Les Crêtes, the inlet just west of the watch-house.

 Follow the path westward until a shallow valley is reached (quite near Mont Hèrault) and a path will take you down to **Baie de la Forge**, a savage cove in which is a splendid *souffleur*, or blow-hole. To see it in action you should be there about 2 hours after low water. The rising tide, on entering the aperture in the rock, forces air out of an upper hole, resulting in a column of spray being ejected, accompanied by a thumping sound. Sunshine produces a rainbow effect. Even when the *souffleur* is idle the place has a wild appeal, though to reach the bay's floor involves climbing down from the blow-hole,

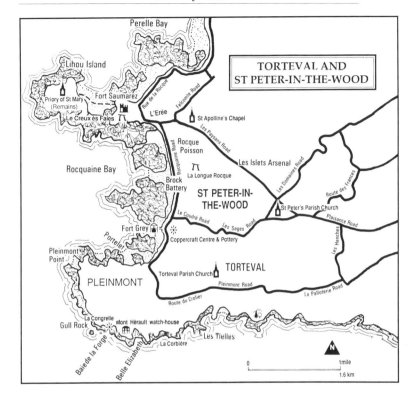

a rather laborious task.

Returning to the cliff path, in a very short while the visitor is confronted by another dramatic piece of nature's handiwork: **La Congrelle** (the Place of Congers), a high-sided gully, water-filled at full tide and with a rough path descending to sea level. From below, the dark, sheer cliffs look distinctly menacing. So does the great German tower on the heights of L'Angle, off which is the sombre stack of the Gull Rock. This is a wonderful region, always dramatic and with a severe beauty unmatched in Guernsey.

Lofty television masts have, as a companion, another stalwart tower built by the Germans. A mile out to sea is something very different: **Les Hanois lighthouse**, which was completed in 1862 and is now automatically operated. Until recently keepers were brought from Portelet harbour, where a Trinity House launch was moored for this purpose. The lighthouse stands about 2 miles from **Pleinmont Point** (said to face a stretch of sea whose limit is America), near which was the so-called 'Haunted House' (in reality another watch-house), that featured in *The Toilers of the Sea*, Victor Hugo's romance. The Germans destroyed most of the building, which was not a handsome one, but they could not kill the magnificence of its setting.

At Pleinmont Point the cliffs come to an end and the track descends to a gentle, grassy amphitheatre, encompassed by rocky heights. Across this greensward the way goes through a gap in the rocks into another, more open, space, where a mound, surrounded by stones, will be noticed. It is Le Table des Pions, around which sat the horsemen's grooms who participated in the cavalcade of La Chevauchée, previously mentioned at the Forest Church. The mound, grass-covered, is surrounded by a ditch, in which rested the *pions'* feet.

A finely paved slipway nearby leads to a stony beach from which, in the past, *vraic* was gathered. Carts, drawn by heavy horses, took it to farms, where it was used as a fertilizer. Today, farmers prefer to buy the artificial variety. Such slipways are common and attractive features of Guernsey beaches. Overlooking the inlet is **Fort** **Pézéries**, an eighteenth-century work whose origins were much earlier. It is in a good state of preservation, with its magazine and gun positions intact. Its cannon doubtless protected this end of Rocquaine Bay from invaders, though its best defences must have been the rocks and racing tides of this wide bight.

Half a mile on, beyond the car park and reached by an attractive path on the road's landward side, is **Portelet harbour**, a most pleasant fishermen's harbour, full of boats and overlooked by Trinity House cottages, trim buildings occupied by lighthouse keepers and their families. Brooding over the scene is the crag of La Varde, standing at the foot of the Zigzag, a road running up to the Torteval Heights. Just past Portelet is the Imperial Hotel, near which Pleinmont-bound buses come to rest.

Pleinmont's attractions are not confined to its coastline. From the cliffs by the television masts is a lane (the Zigzag) running downhill and bordering the Guernsey National Trust's property, **Le Vau de Monel**, its first acquisition. It is a wooded valley of much charm, enjoying fine views of Rocquaine and running down to the Portelet coast road. Alternatively, several other nearby lanes lead there and, on the way, are cottages, little fields, perhaps tethered cows and a quite enchanting rural environment.

By the Rocquaine coast road stands **Fort Grey**, with its whitewashed Martello tower now serving as a landmark. It is enclosed by a high parapet. Originally the ancient Château de Rocquaine, it was the haunt of witches. In 1804, when it was rebuilt, it was renamed after a Guernsey Lieutenant-Governor. In 1976 it was made into a maritime museum, mainly housing relics of west coast shipwrecks. Most certainly it ought to be visited and special note should be made of the paving stones of its batteries.

Just north of the fort a road runs inland, winding its way gently uphill, passing farms and a pumping station. This leads to Les Islets Arsenal (a relic of militia days), standing beside the main road from L'Erée headland to St Peter-in-the-Wood. Opposite is the Coach House Gallery, full of interest. Another worthwhile inland road starts from just north of Fort Grey, leading uphill to Les Clercs and the old house of St Brioc. Before long the spire of Torteval Church becomes visible in pastoral surroundings.

Torteval Church is not a very handsome building and the one it replaced in 1816 was fairer (though it was in poor condition), yet the church should be visited, for, within, it has a simple and endearing quality. One of its bells is the oldest in the island; it was cast in 1432. Lanes abound close by and to 'lose' oneself in them is quite a pleasant experience, since the distances involved in finding one's way to the coast or even the town are short. To be truly lost in Guernsey is almost impossible.

ST PETER-IN-THE-WOOD (*BUS C1 & C2*)

Midway along Rocquaine's sea road is **Brock Battery**, one of the island's numerous defences against a French invasion, and this stands at the boundary of the parishes of Torteval (Guernsey's

Mont Hèrault

smallest) and St Pierre du Bois, to give it its ancient title. A short distance north of the battery is **Rocque Poisson** (a large rock which is a prominent feature on the road's seaward side) and opposite is a lane which, if you proceed eastward and upward, will bring you to Les Paysans Road, flanked by comely farmsteads and the less beautiful school of La Houguette.

Follow this hill and soon, on the right, as the road approaches the summit, you will observe a standing stone in the middle of a field and on private property. It is **La Longue Rocque**, the tallest menhir in Guernsey. Once upon a time a cross stood near it. Legend relates that it was once a cricket bat (no less) used by fairies, and another story tells that a fairy woman carried it ashore in her apron and planted it in the field. She must have been as tough as the stone, for it is llft 6in (3.5m) high from ground level.

Little more than half a mile further along the road (turn right at the Longfrie Hotel) is **St Peter's Parish Church**, with its sturdy tower and wooded setting. Like its fellows, it is mentioned in a charter of

La Congrelle

1030 and must have existed before then, although not in its present form. It is built on a hillside and, within, the upward slope of the floor from west to east is quite pronounced. Among the features not to be missed are the tower arch and the rose window above it, the oil lamps, militia colours and the massive alms box. At the northern entrance gate is a fine mounting block and the war memorial east of the building enhances its beauty. Because of its position, the tower does not seem to be over 100ft (about 33m), but from its summit the enjoyable view endorses its true height. West of the church the main road passes the airport on its way to St Peter Port.

L'Erée is a headland and settlement half a mile north of Brock Battery, dominated by a German tower, superimposed on the much older Fort Saumarez. Walk up the low hill on the promontory and just before reaching the tower look out for an inconspicuous turning on the right. Here, below a mound, is the dolmen of **Le Creux ès Faies**, the Entrance to Fairyland, folklore revealed. In World War II the Germans fortified this area but spared the megalith, as they did the

Coast at L'Erée

Torteval Church

dolmen of La Varde, at L'Ancresse.

Opposite L'Erée Hotel is a green area, La Claire Mare, once used by aircraft before the war. Interesting cottages flank the road and a large car park lies seaward. The beach is extremely popular and L'Erée itself, despite some questionable buildings here and there, retains much of its ancient charm, though its seaside dunes have been obliterated. Buses will take you there, some labelled 'Lihou Island', but they will not go quite as far as that!

From L'Erée's headland the view is broad. South lies the sweep of Rocquaine; north the coast can be seen as far as Grandes Rocques; inland are gentle slopes and, seaward, almost at one's feet, is the isle of **Lihou** (*Bus E1, E2, & K*). One may walk there with ease at low water (preferably at a spring tide, when you can spend longer on it, for a causeway, paved in parts, winds over the rocky

PLACES OF INTEREST
IN TORTEVAL

Baie de la Forge
Savage cove with a splendid
souffleur, or blow-hole. Visits
should be made about 2 hours
after low water.

Fort Grey
Maritime museum on Rocquaine
coast road. Relics of west coast
wrecks housed in ancient fort.
Limited parking.
Originally the haunt of witches,
rebuilt in 1804 and named after
Guernsey Lieutenant-Governor.
(*Bus C1, C2, K*).

Parish Church
Nineteenth century, but
interesting. Attractive countryside
nearby, including cliffs.
(*Bus C1, C2*).

Pleinmont
Headland overlooks Les Hanois
lighthouse. Fort Pézéries and
Table des Pions are a short walk
from bus terminus outside
Imperial Hotel. Parking.
Refreshments. (*Bus C1, C2, K*).

Note: Massive German
fortifications near Pleinmont
Point. Others along Rocquaine
Bay.

shore, flanked by large pools. These rapidly fill when the tide turns
and one must not linger when this happens. A board on the islet
normally advises visitors when it is time to go and it could be
dangerous to disregard it. The causeway can be damp in places. Two
man-made objects stand on this 18-acre isle (roughly 7ha): the scant
remains of **St Mary's Priory** and a well-designed modern dwelling,
standing on the site of a big farmhouse, destroyed when the Germans
chose it as a target for their L'Erée artillery. On the beach close by
seaweed used to be dried on frames and used in the small factory
once adjoining the house. Here iodine was made, but all this was
swept away during the Occupation.

While the Germans spared the priory ruins, wind and weather
have not, and little remains of this remote religious house today. It
was never a large settlement (the islet's size precluded this) and it
was founded in medieval times. It was sequestrated in 1415 as an
alien priory since (like others in Guernsey), it was under the control
of the Abbey of Mont St Michel. It was granted to Eton College from

Fort Grey

L'Erée Bay

then until the Reformation , when the priory was allowed to fall into ruin. What remains has been fully investigated and many valuable discoveries have been made. Various people have rented Lihou from its owner, the Crown, and today its tenants are the Hon and Mrs Robin Berwick. The public are free to enjoy Lihou's quietude and to swim in the deep rock pool at its western end. Over the reefs is Lihoumel islet. All is attractive, with a strong feeling of being 'out of this world', but remember the tide and return while the going is good. The causeway was probably built by the monks and was especially appreciated by carters of *vraic* (seaweed).

Back on the Guernsey mainland, follow the coast road to **Perelle Bay** (*Bus E1, E2 & K*), within a mile of L'Erée. It is a rocky place, scarcely a popular resort, yet for the marine biologist and all who enjoy a shore scramble, it has much to offer. A restaurant stands close by.

Practically opposite is a lane, running west. It passes Le Catioroc, a former watch-house which has now been transformed

PLACES OF INTEREST IN ST PETER-IN-THE-WOOD

Coach House Gallery
Les Islets.
Fine collection housed in former
barns. Occasional exhibitions.
(*Bus C2*).

La Corbière
Striking headland. Havre de Bon
Repos below. Parking (limited).
About $\frac{1}{2}$ mile from nearest bus
stop. (*Bus C1, C2*).

L'Erée
Fort Saumarez and Creux ès
Faies dolmen (inconspicuous)
on headland overlooking Lihou
Island. Popular beach. Refresh-
ments. Parking. Bus terminus for
Lihou Island. (*Bus C1, C2, K*).

La Longue Rocque
Rocquaine.
Guernsey's tallest standing

stone. On private land, but
visible from the road.

Parish Church
Noted for sloping floor and fine
proportions. Interesting
churchyard and surroundings.
(*Bus C2*).

Perelle
Rocky bay. Inland is St Apolline's
Chapel and on coast Le Trepied
dolmen. Refreshments and
parking at Perelle.
(*Bus E1, E2, K*).

Rocquaine Bay
Extensive bay extending from
Portelet harbour to L'Erée.
Hinterland of interest. Opposite
Fort Grey is Coppercraft, open
daily.
(*Bus C1, C2, K*).

into something much bigger, and has a German-built tower. The lane, Le Chemin du Roi (of great antiquity), becomes an agreeable grassy way, flanked by massive boulders here and there, and with the adjoining land owned by the local National Trust. At the seaward end, near a German defence work, is **Le Trepied dolmen**, once the haunt of witches, if not the devil himself, where unholy revels took place on Friday nights. The coast road lies below and offshore is the minute islet of **Dom Hue**, accessible at low tide. Here, declares tradition, was once a hermit's cell and some traces of it survive, perhaps.

If one returns to Perelle, only a short distance along the shore road, one should certainly visit **St Apolline's Chapel**, an ancient place of worship, standing on the left of the main road, Grande Rue,

Perelle Bay

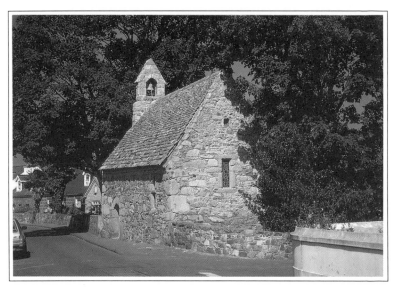

St Apolline's Chapel

and reached by turning left at Les Rouvets. Built in 1392, it looks much older. It was sympathetically restored in 1980, when its bellcote was renewed. The roof is of Cumberland slate and the newly grassed area enhances the chapel's appearance. Within are traces of frescoes and the simple furnishings are in the best of taste. It is still used on occasions. The chapel was acquired by the States of Guernsey in 1873, at a time when it was used as a stable. It was thus the island's first ancient monument. Actually, Perelle is within the parish of St Saviour, but it is convenient to include the area in this section.

St Saviour's and St Andrew's

ST SAVIOUR'S

Of all Guernsey's country churches, St Saviour's Church (Bus D1 and D2), is the largest, and many may declare it to be the best. The building's graceful tower, its proportions and its setting add to the attractions of a particularly delightful parish. The church has something of a French flavour in its style and there is an element of craftsmanship about it, often lacking elswhere, and reminiscent of that found in the Town Church. The spire rises to a height of 103ft and it is capped by a fine weathercock, above a modern clock. During the Occupation this tower served the Germans as an observation post and beneath the church they built vast tunnels, which remain, though fortunately they seem not to have affected its foundations. They are now open to the public.

In the churchyard there is much to see. Its north-eastern entrance is flanked by a Christianised menhir, on which a cross has been deeply incised on the outer face. There is another at the back of the stone pillar. In the little paved lane leading to the cemetery from the south-west is a stone bench, once the meeting place of the court of Fief Jean du Gailliard. Some of the gravestones repay examination, especially that covering the remains of those lost in the cutter *Pitt* off Perelle in 1819.

The church can be reached by bus and, having inspected it, one should walk down to the coast via the reservoir. Start by descending the hill to Sous l'Eglise ('Below the Church') and follow the narrow Rue de l'Eglise to a crossroads. Bear right to reach one end of the 240 million gallon reservoir. Rue du Moulin climbs uphill to the main road; then turn left, downhill, for a brief distance, passing Mont Varouf school en route. Soon, on the left, is an approach to the massive dam and it is an interesting experience to cross it by footpath. The reservoir itself is a beauty spot, a haunt of birds, and a stroll around its perimeter track is a worthwhile exercise. The reservoir occupies the site of a charming, drowned, valley and in times of drought the ruins of buildings emerge. The vast undertaking was completed in 1947.

The cliffs near Les Tielles

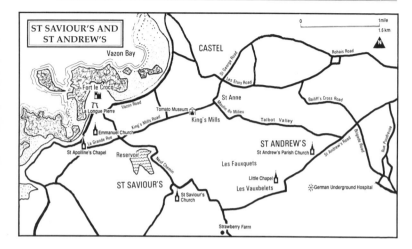

On the far (western) side of the dam, turn right and then right again. You will thus reach **Le Mont Saint** (The Holy Hill), reputed to have been the haunt of fairies, from which a pleasant road runs almost due west to Richmond, on the coast. Its fort stands above the western extremity of Vazon Bay, below which is the privately-owned Fort Le Crocq. On its north side is a menhir, **La Longue Pierre**, (9ft, 3m) tall, with, possibly, a fellow of equal age nearby.

In upper St Saviour's, round about the church, are many narrow lanes, most pleasant to walk through, even if, at times, a car or two may be encountered. The possibility of becoming lost temporarily is, to some extent, offset by the conspicuous church tower, visible from many points. Notice the fine old stone farmhouses and their massive outbuildings. Occasionally mounting blocks, well built granite archways, stone chimney stacks and stout walls can be seen. Here is a breath of the country, peaceful (save for the occasional aircraft) and affording glimpses of the celebrated island cattle, often tethered, in order to make the most of the limited pasture. Glasshouses are visible at times, unlovely, yet to be tolerated, since horticulture plays so big a part in the island's economy.

Lower St Saviour's is equally engaging. Its shoreline has already been seen at Perelle and Vazon, but there is another aspect not to be missed. To enjoy it return to the church and walk a little way

Underground Museum in an old German tunnel, St Saviours

eastward along a road flanked by wide grass verges. These are **Les Buttes**, once an archery ground ('butts') used by medieval militiamen. Continue along this pleasant highway (which becomes Rue des Prevosts) until it turns abruptly right. Then ignore the main road and take a lane ahead (Rue des Boulains). Disregard the first left-hand turn and take the second, which soon becomes an enchanting valley way, ending just past a former watermill, Moulin de Haut, whose house stands in a lovely garden, with a steep hillside behind it. At the main road turn left to approach the **King's Mills** (Bus E1 & E2), where several watermills once stood beside the stream. Here is one of Guernsey's few villages, even though it lacks a church and pub, as well as shops. Practically all its buildings are beautiful and the enfolding hills shield them from bad weather. It is, indeed, a glorious place, reached by bus, but better appreciated if approached on foot. An important waterworks station in no way spoils its good looks.

A right turn at the main road leads to the lower end of Talbot valley,

An old water pump at Strawberry Farm

Guernsey is famous for its tomatoes

another countryside gem, but this is considered in the Castel section. From the King's Mills the road runs westward, but leave it at the second turning right after passing the Hotel Fleur du Jardin, and follow a track across a flat expanse, known as La Grande Mare. This was once a marsh. In a short distance is Vazon Bay, one of the largest and most popular in Guernsey. In prehistoric times a forest existed below the expanse of sand and occasionally traces of this are exposed.

ST ANDREW'S *(BUS D1 &D2)*

This is the only Guernsey parish without a coastline, but despite this, it has much to offer. It is rural in character and the upper reaches of Talbot Valley are near the **Parish Church**, a small but most appealing building beside a busy road. Originally it was styled

PLACES OF INTEREST IN ST SAVIOUR'S

Fort Le Crocq and La Longue Pierre
Menhir below Fort Richmond, on headland. (*Bus E1, E2, K*).

Parish Church
Guernsey's largest country church. Imposing tower, well proportioned building. Menhir at eastern entrance of interesting churchyard. (*Bus D1, D2*).

Silversmith
Bruce Russell, workshop and showrooms, Le Gran. (*Bus D1, D2*).

Strawberry Farm
Les Issues.
Fruit grown under glass, also wood carving. Refreshments. (*Bus D1, D2*).

Ecclesia Sancti Andreae de Putente Pomeria (Church of St Andrew of the Sloping Orchard) and its antiquity, though undated, is beyond dispute. Of all Guernsey's places of worship, perhaps this is one of the most resembling an English village church. The rectory beside it is handsome, though the adjacent road, Rue des Morts, has a deadly ring about it!

Barely half a mile west, by road, is another religious place of far greater interest to most people than the parish church. It is La Grotte, the famed '**Little Chapel**' of **Les Vauxbelets**, a large and attractive estate where once stood a school. The chapel was started in 1923 by one of the brothers of the former religious house administering the school and farm, and it has been added to ever since. It is largely made of fragments of china, pottery and shells and has a curiously attractive appearance, appealing strongly to most visitors to Guernsey. It is, however, ironical that they should ignore the church in favour of something far less enduring.

Another 'attraction' is the former **German Underground Hospital**, located in La Vassalerie road, reached from the church by a turning (left) just beyond St Andrew's Hotel. This forbidding place has an appeal for those anxious to see Occupation relics of all kinds and certainly it is impressive, albeit in rather a morbid fashion.

Much more cheerful is a short walk around the perimeter of Les

PLACES OF INTEREST IN ST ANDREW'S

Parish Church
Attractive, in rural setting.
(*Bus D1, D2*).

German Underground Hospital,
close to church.
Gloomy but impressive. Open
daily.

Les Vauxbelets
Few hundred yards west of

former hospital. Its 'Little Chapel'
is a great tourist attraction.
Grounds also worth seeing.
Limited parking.
(*Bus D1, D2*).

Botanical Gardens
La Villiaze
(*Bus D1, D2*).

Vauxbelets. Leave the Little Chapel and walk westward, uphill, and take the first turning right. It passes the old house of Les Grands Guilliaumes and wends its way to Candie Road, where one may turn left and visit the most attractive Fauxquets Valley, or, continuing past Les Vauxbelets property, turn right and then right again along La Mare Road. In no time the main gates of the estate are reached.

On the fringe of St Andrew's parish is St Pierre Park Hotel, situated at the foot of Rohais Road and occupying the site of a former Roman Catholic school, named 'Vimiera'. It is one of Guernsey's largest and most modern hotels, standing in 40 acres (16 ha) of parkland and landscaped gardens, in which is a 9-hole golf course. It is, indeed, an impressive feature in the island scene, noticed by passers-by, bound from St Peter Port to the west coast.

Little Chapel, Les Vauxbelets

Castel Parish

This is Guernsey's largest parish (2,525 acres or about 1,000ha) and one of its most interesting. It stands on the edge of high ground, known as the Upper Parishes, overlooking the flat regions of the north. Its name is derived from the castle believed to have stood on the site of the parish church, whose official name is St Marie du Castro. The castle was Le Château du Grand Sarrasin, one Geoffroi, perhaps a Danish pirate who made the island his headquarters at some unrecorded date.

The Parish Church commands a magnificent prospect, and the site would have been ideal as a defence work or observation post. Once again, a Christian place of worship was built in an erstwhile pagan stronghold, since, in the cemetery, stands a statue menhir, perhaps a female goddess, though less comely than her sister at St Martin's. It was discovered under the chancel floor in 1878 and was set up near the west porch. The flat stones at its feet were originally sited at the northern end of the churchyard and here, until a century or so ago, tho officials of La Cour du Fief Lihou used to assemble, a reminder of feudal Guernsey.

The menhir is 6ft 6in high (about 2m) and one of its breasts has been mutilated, possibly at the time when the menhir was removed from its original position and concealed in the church. It is thought to be more ancient than the St Martin's figure and may date from the tenth century BC. Close by is a handsome red granite trough on which are carved two faces, resembling the sun and moon. The carving may have been executed in the sixteenth century and the trough came from Les Fontaines farm, near the church.

Folklore suggests that the intended site for the church was at Les Eturs, near the centre of the parish (the present one is at the edge of it), but the fairies, whose resort it was, removed the stones left by the builders every night, so that, in despair, Les Eturs was abandoned in favour of the present position. Partly because of its situation, the parish was also served by three medieval chapels: St Anne's (at the King's Mills), St George (to be dealt with later in this section) and St Germain (close to St George). Much more modern is St Matthew's

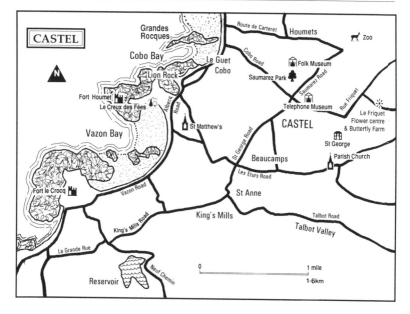

Church, at Albecq, close to Cobo, a Victorian building and of considerable charm.

In some respects, the exterior of the Castel Church resembles those of the Vale, St Martin's and the Forest, for each has a spire and, for that matter, the site of each was associated with pagan worship. The building is more interesting within than without. The tower is supported by four stout columns and under the bell-loft is some fine groining. A 'squint' pierces the south-east column (it gave worshippers a view of the high altar when it stood in the north chancel) and, with the same purpose in mind, for lepers attending mass in the churchyard (so it is believed) there is a 'low-side window' on the south side of the nave. Close to it is part of a priest's door.

Of special interest are the frescoes, dating from the thirteenth century, on the north side and high up. One depicts the Last Supper, another is of a hunting scene and the third could represent St Thomas à Becket. They may well be contemporary with those of St Apolline's Chapel. There is an element of mystery as to the origin of these wall paintings, as there is in the presence of a great carved stone over the fireplace in Castel rectory, below the church. It is considered to be a fifteenth-century lintel, far older than the present rectory, but perhaps from the original one.

A good place from which to begin a Castel walk is from the church. So proceed westward, soon passing the Fair Field, with a stone obelisk in the middle. It recalls the days when cattle shows were held here and, indeed, when a fair took place nearby in the Middle Ages. The memorial is to Nicholas Le Beir, one-time secretary of the Royal Guernsey Agricultural Society; it was erected in 1860. Practically opposite is a lane, La Ruette des Touillets; go down here, turn left and then right (La Ruette du Ponchez). A further turn left goes downhill (via Rue du Torval) to Route des Talbots — **Talbot Valley** (*Bus E1, & E2*), in fact.

Rightly, this is considered to be one of the best bits of countryside in Guernsey, although a century ago there were many others equally attractive. It extends from Les Poidevins (near St Andrew's Church) to the King's Mills and it is flanked by low hills, gracious buildings and a stream, once serving several mills. One of them survives in a restored state and should be seen. It is at **Les Niaux** and it can be reached by walking up the valley road for a few yards and then turning right, crossing the stream to the massive waterwheel. The mill-house is handsome and the setting is one of much charm.

Return to the valley road and walk downhill, a very gentle descent. Soon, on the right, is a cottage and behind it is the **Ron Short Walk**. On no account should this be missed: it is a small but important possession of the National Trust of Guernsey, one of whose staunchest supporters was the late Mr Short. A path runs in a semi-circle past the garden, and emerges, through a copse, a little further downhill. The quiet main road soon bears left and rises a little, passing an unusual old stone gateway leading to Le Groignet estate, where vines are cultivated.

Soon is the turning (left) off which is Le Moulin de Haut and on the approach to the King's Mills (see also pages 133-5) the house of Le Moulin de Milieu will be seen. The waterworks stands on the site of Le Moulin de Bas. Originally, this area was known as Les Grands Moulins (the Big Mills) and part of it is in St Saviour's parish and has been described in that section.

Castel Parish Church

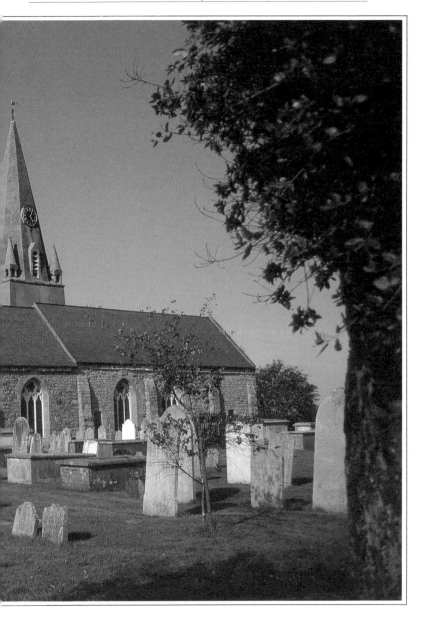

PLACES OF INTEREST IN CASTEL

Cobo, Grandes Rocques and Vazon
Some of Guernsey's most popular bays, each adjoining the other on west coast. (*Bus El, E2, F, K for Vazon; F,G,K. for Cobo; Hl,H2,G,K for Grandes Rocques*). Refreshments, public conveniences and parking at all these bays.

Friquet Flower Centre and Butterfly Farm
Much beauty on display, especially in butterfly section. Shop and refreshments. (*Bus F,G*).

Parish Church
Statue menhir at entrance. Much to see within. Glorious view from churchyard, which is itself worth seeing. (*Bus El, E2*).

Saumarez Park
Home for the elderly (ground floor), open mornings. Folk Museum near mansion. Attractive grounds, open at all times. Refreshments. Parking. Large childrens adventure playground (*Bus F*).

Telephone Museum
Cobo Road.
Small but fascinating equipment on view and in use locally since 1898. (*Bus F*).

Talbot Valley
Beautiful valley with mill stream. Restored mill and waterwheel.

Having duly admired the many excellent houses and gardens of this attractive place go past the water treatment plant and walk up Rue de la Porte, with the estate of that name on the left and the site of St Anne's Chapel on the right. At a crossroads, with the main road to Vazon running downhill, cross over, and on the left is the fine old house of **La Houguette**, standing back from the road in its delectable garden. Its name denotes 'The Little Hill', for 'La Hougue' means the large hill, names often encountered in the island.

Just beyond a red granite Methodist church, Les Deslisles, is the main entrance to the large and lovely estate of **St George**, which is sometimes open to the public. At the gates is the feudal court-house of Fief Le Comte and in the grounds are the scanty ruins of St George's Chapel, medieval and feudal, since its court once met there. When the chapel was demolished in the eighteenth century

Waterwheel at Talbot Valley

(having served as a school until one for the parish was built elsewhere), the meeting place was transferred to the present building. Beside the chapel's remains is the Holy Well of St George, surmounted by a cross and a hood, in which is a niche for the alms of those who sought the well's alleged curative powers.

This was once a very holy place, if legends are to be believed. Here, in times long past, St George and St Patrick met. The former gave his blessing to the area now bearing his name and bestowed curative properties to its well. The latter drove out all 'harmful creatures' from Guernsey. Legends tell of people being healed of ailments by using its waters and having faith in their powers. Once again, a chapel was built near a prehistoric site, for the now destroyed Rocquees Boeufs stood near St George and it was probably a menhir. The well, moreover, may have had magical associations and La Croix St Georges (St George's Cross) was erected to destroy them, just as the pagan fountain was 'converted' into a holy well. The grounds of St George are as attractive as the house in their midst, a grey stone building behind which is considerably older. Further along the road is another entrance, with a handsome archway over it.

On the right of the road, but at a higher level, is Les Beaucamps School, standing on the site of the Royal Guernsey Militia's training camp. The huts comprising it were built in 1900 and ceased to be used when the Militia was disbanded in 1940. The present school dates from 1959 and was opened by HRH Princess Margaret. It can be seen at close quarters if one turns right at the crossroads and follows Les Beaucamps Road until the school is reached. This thoroughfare passes the estate of Les Beaucamps, with its big house surrounded by fields and continues to Rue du Préel, running back to Castel Church.

Alternatively, at the crossroads beyond St George walk down the hill, flanked on the left by a splendid stone wall. It borders **La Haye du Puits**, an ancient and stately home with a garden as attractive as the house. Once the residence of the Le Marchants (a distinguished Guernsey family), it has a French appearance and a glimpse of it may be obtained from its entrance arch, bearing the Le Marchant arms.

It is remarkable that this part of Castel parish is rich in big estates, probably due to the excellence of its soil. Almost rubbing shoulders with each other are St George, Les Beaucamps, La Haye du Puits and Saumarez Park, with the somewhat smaller property of Les Mourains (opposite the park) added for good measure. Of these, only Saumarez Park is open to the public.

The gracious estate of **Saumarez Park** (*Bus F*), is easily reached by bus and parking is available near the house. Formerly it was the country seat of Lord de Saumarez, in whose family it remained for nearly 200 years. Originally it belonged to a branch of the Le Marchants, from whom it was transferred by inheritance. The arms of both families grace one of the gateways. The property was considerably enlarged in the early part of the twentieth century and once included Japanese buildings, erected by workmen from Japan, where the fourth baron was in the Diplomatic Service. He was also responsible for the attractive bridge crossing Route de Carteret, linking the park with the Mare de Carteret property north of it.

During his absence abroad, Saumarez Park became the residence of the Lieutenant-Governor. This was at a time when

La Haye du Puits

Guernsey had no official Government House. Lord Saumarez, in his old age, received Edward, Prince of Wales, on his visit to the island in 1935. The baron died in 1937 and in the following year the estate was purchased by the States of Guernsey. During the German Occupation it served as States Offices. For many years it has been a home for the aged and bears the name of the Hostel of St John.

The grounds are open to the public and are most attractive. There are fine trees and shrubs and an interesting fishing hut stands beside the small lake. There is also a children's playground and during the summer various shows are held in the park. In August the Guernsey Battle of Flowers is staged here, a major attraction. Refreshments are available near the house.

Adjoining the residence is the **Guernsey Folk Museum**, administered by the National Trust of Guernsey in conjunction with La Société Guernesiaise. It is of major importance and houses an admirable collection of farm vehicles and implements, a reconstructed cider press, a realistic-looking Old Guernsey Kitchen, as well as numerous other reminders of the past, with emphasis on the countryside. In summer *Le Viar Marchi* takes place in the grounds and attracts many visitors and islanders. Among its entertainments are folk dancing, the practice of rural crafts, much good old Guernsey food and a wide variety of souvenirs. This is a National Trust enterprise well worth supporting.

A WALK FROM SAUMAREZ PARK TO GRANDES ROCQUES

It is a good idea to make this excursion in the morning, when the ground floor of the house is open to the public. Having seen its treasures (including de Saumarez heirlooms), there is time to visit the Folk Museum before leaving the park via the main gates, on the Cobo road, and passing the estate of Le Pouquelah on the right. Turn right along Ruette de Saumarez (which skirts the park) and at a house named 'Manor View' go straight ahead (north) along Ruette de la Tour, a country lane which soon provides a view of Cobo on the left. Fields are on the opposite side and soon a small grey stone tower will be seen, a 'folly' of the de Saumarez family.

Near this tower (close to a small reservoir) enter a bridle path and follow it as it gradually winds downhill. The States of Guernsey, with good taste and ingenuity, have created a nature trail and place of tranquility which is admirable. Amid a wealth of trees and shrubs, there are traces of old walls and a disused quarry. Here and there are seats, some enjoying wide views, a picnic area and a rockery in the glen.

The path emerges on to Route de Carteret at a point where the de Saumarez foot bridge spans the road. It was built so that members of the family proceeding from the house to their property in the Mare de Carteret area should not be obliged to cross the roadway — at least, so it is said. This bridge may be used. Across the way the path goes past Mare de Carteret School and the remains of a small canal — more de Saumarez work, of course — survive. At the tennis courts bear left, after crossing the canal, and follow the track to the coast road. Grandes Rocques and the buses are not very far away.

LE GUET, VAZON AND GRANDES ROCQUES

Among the Castel properties formerly in de Saumarez ownership is **Le Guet** (The Sentinel) (*Bus F, G & K*), a distinctive hill overlooking Cobo Bay and now the property of the States. Today it is so densely wooded that the ancient watch-house giving the hill its name is almost invisible. The firs were planted about 50 years ago and seem never to have been thinned. This is a pity, for they rob the hill of much of its former character; the fire risk, too, must be high.

The watch-house and adjacent battery were part of the anti- French fortifications. A beacon was held in readiness, to be fired at sight of the foe and it is interesting to reflect that among the air raid precautions of 1939 was a siren which was installed at Le Guet. In 1940, when the Germans bombed the island, it sounded the 'Alert', but the 'All Clear' was never heard. One may walk up to the walls of the watch-house, but entry is barred, because of past vandalism. It is quite a small building, but the view it commands is vast. German defences add to the hill's history, but not to its natural beauty. Below the watch-house is a steep quarry face, running to the coast road, beside which stands a disused powder magazine, one of many around the island shores. Paths connect Le Guet with the coast road, with Cobo just around the corner.

Albecq can be reached inland from Le Guet or from the shore road. It comprises a collection of modern dwellings amid which stands St Matthew's Church, attractively built of Cobo stone in Norman style. It dates from 1854 and it was a child, Marianne Carey, who was responsible for it. She persuaded her father to build a place of worship for the benefit of the fishermen living nearby. He agreed and the family raised most of the £3,600 needed! The neighbouring vicarage harmonizes well with the church's fabric.

The bay of Albecq (hardly a good bathing place, though it looks well at a full tide) lies on the northern flank of the Houmet peninsula, itself forming the north boundary of **Vazon Bay** (*Bus E1, E2, F & K*). This headland is a fine piece of coastline, with its red rocks (and how vivid they are at sunset!), fortifications and that echo of folklore in its cave: **Le Creux des Fées**, another portal of fairyland. There are several legends associated with the cave, which lies a short distance north of Fort Houmet. Its adjacent creek looks its best at high tide,

Le Friquet Butterfly Farm and Flower Centre

Vazon Bay

Surfers at Vazon Bay, Fort Houmet in the background

when its deep, clear water is admirable for swimming and diving
While the creek is unmistakable, the cavern may take a little finding,
though it is very near and is always accessible at low tide. A rough
fence encloses an opening in its roof.

In its present form, **Fort Houmet** is about 200 years old. It was one ✳
of the few old coastal defences to be used by the garrison in modern
times, although it was seldom occupied for long periods. Like its
fellows, it was not overlooked by the Germans. In 1955 its barracks
were destroyed, since they were unsightly and dangerously ruined,
and in 1982 considerable restoration work on the fort has vastly
improved its appearance. Like others of its kind, it may be inspected
without formality, although motorists must park a respectful distance
away.

Where the headland merges with the coastline stands another of ✳
Guernsey's so-called Martello towers. In fact, the fort's tower is a true
Martello and a comparison will reveal their differences. Both are of
the local stone and merge into the landscape in a way the harsh

German concrete structures fail to do, although gradually even these are becoming slightly more mellow than they used to be.

The **Cobo** area has been greatly built upon in post-war years and some of its charm has suffered in consequence. The bay, like Vazon, nevertheless remains a great favourite among visitors and residents, since it is excellent for bathers and surfers (when conditions permit) and it is beloved by sun-bathers and all who enjoy rock scrambles. To be in this region at sunset is to behold an unforgettable spectacle.

An easy walk is to proceed from Vazon to **Grandes Rocques** (*Bus H1, H2, K & G*), via Cobo, of course. Despite the traffic it is enjoyable, since a pedestrian path hugs the shore. On the way refreshment places abound. The sands of Saline Bay, north of Cobo itself, are very popular and so is the Grandes Rocques headland, with its masses of granite and fortifications. It is easily reached by bus and there is ample parking space near one of the most attractive-looking hotels in the island. It was off this headland that two of the most spectacular of Guernsey wrecks occurred. They were the giant ore carrier *Elwood Mead* in 1973, and the oil rig *Orion* in 1978. Eventually, both vessels were salvaged.

On the northern side of Grandes Rocques is **Port Soif**, an almost circular bay, very sandy and with two rocky islets to explore. The Castel parish boundary ends here, but one can stray into the Vale to see Portinfer Bay (excellent for surfing at low tide) and its rocky neighbour, Pécquéries. A good path over the dunes links these bays for the stroller and there is parking on the headlands. Soon sandy Port Grat is reached and it is surprising that so few seem to go there. Inland, the terrain is not inspiring, but this cannot be said of Martello-crowned Rousse, the headland bordering Grand Havre. Walk along its pier, wander among the boats at low tide, pause on the battery and admire the bay when it is water filled, then, near Hotel Houmet du Nord, take the bus back into town.

Herm

About three-quarters of a square mile in area, Herm, geographically speaking, is a miniature Guernsey. Both have high land in the south and an area of low-lying territory northward. Another factor common to both is their wealth of prehistoric remains, mainly in the north of the two islands. Herm lies 3 miles (about 6km) from Guernsey and a few hundred yards north of Jethou, the passage of La Percée separating them. The stretch of water between Guernsey and Herm is the Little Russel and that between Herm and Sark is the Great Russel.

Since the States of Guernsey purchased it from the Crown in 1946, it has become a mecca not only for the visitor but for the islander also. The island's proximity to Guernsey, the ease with which it may be reached, the delight of the passage and, above all, the charm and physical appeal of this little gem of an island have all contributed to its popularity. However, despite this popularity and thanks largely to the wisdom of its tenant, Major Peter Wood, the allure of Herm remains untarnished.

Why did primitive man choose this small place for his sepulchre? Why, indeed, did this choice also apply to its neighbours? Was there some special sanctity about diminutive islands that prompted him to make them his last resting place? For assuredly these Stone Age monuments did not merely commemorate the illustrious dead of their respective islands, for their size and number argue otherwise. Almost certainly they were the tombs of celebrities who were brought from what is now the French mainland, and the reason for this relatively ambitious undertaking is likely to remain an eternal enigma.

Another, much younger, memorial is **St Tugual's Chapel**, on the summit of the hill overlooking the harbour. Its origin is uncertain, although its antiquity is undoubted. Precisely who the saint was is as uncertain as his or her sex. Perhaps it was built in the sixth century by St Magloire, when he founded a religious house in Sark and perhaps a chapel in Guernsey. It was standing in 1186, if it is assumed that the Herm church mentioned in a Bull of Pope Urban III is the building in question. Here might have dwelt a hermit, although Herm's name, though similar, had no connection with him, since it is

Herm Harbour

said to mean deserted or uncultivated land.

From time to time monks have inhabited Herm and even as late as 1881 they were there for a brief while. The device of the island incorporates three monks in its design, although this badge is quite modern. Doubtless, St Tugual's Chapel was in use periodically, though not always for religious purposes. In 1913, when Prince Blucher was the tenant, it was restored and became a private chapel. Today it is still a place of worship and its condition and appearance are admirable.

By 1600 the island had become a hunting ground for the Governors of Guernsey, the prey being deer and rabbits. The deer were surely imported for that purpose. Doubtless Herm must have had a permanent population, albeit a small one, but by 1656 Peter Heylin, the historian, recorded that its inhabitants were 'pheasants and good plentie conies' (rabbits).

The value of Herm granite was appreciated in the nineteenth century, when quarrying was undertaken on a fairly large scale. Excavations were at La Rosière (near the present landing steps), at Le Monceau (a hill north of the harbour) and on the common. A considerable number of men were employed in this industry, for which accommodation had to be provided.

The work extended to the neighbouring islet of **Crevichon** (an offshoot of Jethou) and barges were used to remove the stone. A harbour was built at Herm and the enterprise seemed to be lucrative. The excellence of the granite was undoubted as the steps of St Paul's Cathedral prove. Herm's population in the 1830s rose to about 400 and among the buildings erected was a small lock-up, still standing in the grounds of the White House Hotel, itself a product of industrial Herm. As well as quarrying there was an attempt to mine copper on the cliffs above La Rosière landing, but this was not a successful venture financially.

Unhappily, a monolith, **La Pierre aux Rats**, standing at the extremity of the common, was destroyed by the quarrymen and as this had served as a seamark for centuries, the outcry at its destruction led the company to build the present pillar, still bearing the name of the ancient standing stone. The industry gradually declined, partly because of the remoteness of the island from the granite's destinations, and perhaps because of the volume of stone exported from Guernsey and Alderney in the last century. After the building of St Peter Port's New Harbour the demand for Herm granite ceased, and its quarries and other works were abandoned.

Various wealthy tenants resided in Herm during the latter half of the last century and they effected certain changes, notably in the vicinity of **The Manor**, a ponderous pile on the island's spine. A farm was established, the quarrymen's dwellings were improved and the marks of Herm's heavy industry were, to some degree, effaced. Prince Blücher von Wahlstatt was the most opulent of the tenants, but his tenure ended in 1914 when, as a German, he was interned. During his tenancy he introduced wallabies to the island.

For a while in World War I a small garrison was stationed there and in 1920 Compton Mackenzie, the author, rented both Herm and Jethou from the Crown. Visitors were permitted to land and walk to the Shell Beach, but no further. They would have been barred completely had not the novelist needed their landing fees. His book, *Fairy Gold*, is charmingly set in Herm and Jethou, albeit under ficticious names. In 1923 Mackenzie moved residence to Jethou, selling his lease to Sir Percival Perry who, incidentally, established a post office in Herm in 1925. He lived at the White House and remained there until the outbreak of World War II.

Although the Germans did not fortify Herm they used it as an exercise ground and a place of recreation. The island was cultivated in some measure by the Guernsey States, and cattle were grazed there. Caretakers resided on the island as well as Germans (who did not garrison it permanently) and in 1943 a British raiding force landed there. Buildings were inspected but, at the time, they found neither Germans nor civilians in Herm. Late in 1945, Guernsey's Lieutenant-Governor, Lieutenant-General Sir Philip Neame, VC, spent several days' holiday there and enjoyed it so much that he declared it to be 'the nearest approach to Fairyland I have ever seen'. A year later the Guernsey States bought the island for £15,000 and their first tenant was Mr. A.G. Jefferies, whose task to repair 5 years of neglect was a formidable one. It proved too much for him and in 1949 Major Wood began his tenancy, which has lasted for very many happy years for all concerned. His labours have resulted in Herm remaining as

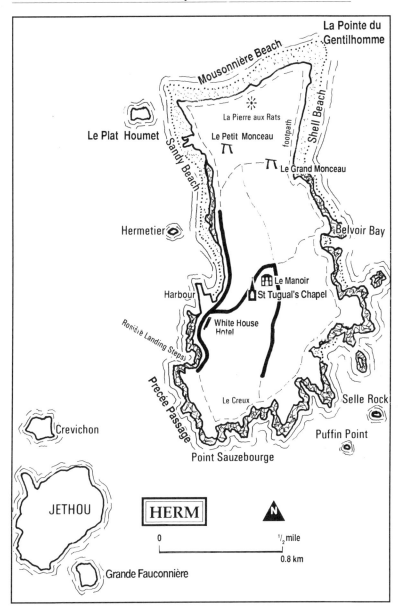

La Pointe du Gentilhomme

Mousonnière Beach

Shell Beach

La Pierre aux Rats

Le Plat Houmet

Sandy Beach

footpath

Le Petit Monceau

Le Grand Monceau

Belvoir Bay

Hermetier

Le Manoir

St Tugual's Chapel

Harbour

White House Hotel

Rosière Landing Steps

Selle Rock

Precée Passage

Le Creux

Puffin Point

Point Sauzebourge

Crevichon

JETHOU

HERM

N

0   ½ mile
           0.8 km

Grande Fauconnière

attractive as it was when it was a rich man's paradise.

An excellent service of launches enables visitors to enjoy Herm to the full, and they can spend a long and rewarding day there. The boats leave at prominently marked places around St Peter Port harbour and the journey is most interesting. Ships in port are passed at close quarters, passengers observe vessels large and small in the Little Russel. The launches proceed close to Bréhon Tower, a massive fortification looking medieval, but in fact dating from the last century. It saw little military service, though the Germans used it as an anti-aircraft battery. It belongs to the States and its main purpose today is to serve as a maritime mark and to provide the site with a flashing light after dark.

Launches normally encircle Jethou as they approach Herm and passengers obtain a close view of this private island, still owned by the Crown but let to a tenant, who does not admit the public to his domain, though this has not always been so.

Landing at Herm depends on the tide. If it is low, the launch will stop at La Rosière Steps; when there is sufficient water the harbour will be used. Normally one uses each landing place on a day trip. The distance between them is negligible. Having landed at the steps, in order to reach the harbour, shops and the island hub, turn left and walk along a coastal path.

It is then that the peace of Herm is first appreciated. The sounds of traffic are confined to the occasional aircraft, a passing launch and perhaps an island truck. Motor vehicles scarcely exist, like bicycles; on Herm one walks because it is so small. How better to see an island whose main attraction is its peace and quiet?

The White House is one of the most desirable hotels in the Channel Islands. It is of just the right size, its comfort and cuisine are renowned, and to stay there is to experience good cheer and serenity. For those less fortunate, its Ship Restaurant provides all that a day visitor needs, a quality shared by the Mermaid Inn, nearby. This stands in an attractive courtyard, where one may rest, eat, and drink. Opposite are the public conveniences, also available between the Shell Beach and Belvoir Bay.

Herm's boutiques have a special quality. Of fairly recent date, they are comparatively small, but so varied are their wares and so well are they displayed that they seem quite spacious. Souvenirs abound and there is room to sit outside and write postcards or merely regard the splendid view seawards. Some visitors seem to stray little further than this tiny village, but Herm warrants more attention than that!

The sturdy stone pier of the harbour has upon it an ancient crane, which is a relic of the granite trade, and a more modern section accommodates a few pleasure craft.

At this point, there is a choice of routes. One may walk northwards, to **Shell Beach**, or ascend the lovely, tree-lined hill, leading to St Tugual's Chapel, and the way to Belvoir Bay, the farm, camp site and other places, all worth seeing. It is largely a matter of time and inclination, and the day's temperature may well govern one's choice. For those with a day in front of them, a walk around the island is to be recommended. For those not so active, a stroll to the Shell Beach and, perhaps, over the common, gives a reasonably good impression of the island.

Walk northwards, along a flat, rather sandy path, the sea on the loft, and on the other hand a gentle hillside, often with Herm's large and handsome herd of cattle grazing there, The **'Fisherman's' Cottage'** is most attractive and opposite is Hermetier, an islet which may be visited at low tide. One could easily proceed along the beach, but perhaps the track is preferable, since the shelly sand becomes a little trying on the feet.

Above 'Fisherman's Cottage' is Le Monceau, a wooded hill partly quarried. Soon a little cemetery on the left is reached. A cross stands over it and there is a solitary inscription: 'In memory of K.W. Conden, aged 2 years. R. Mansfield, aged 23 years. Died April 18-'. One can read no more. How these died and why they rest here is unknown, it would seem. There is a tradition that they were cholera victims; perhaps they were residents.

Before lies the common, and on its green, undulating surface is much of interest. Chief attraction, probably, are the Neolithic graves. Some are to be seen on the slopes of **Le Petit Monceau**, a truly delightful hillock on which flat stones prove admirable resting places. Another ancient grave stands beside the path which branches right and leads to the Shell Beach. High above is **Le Grand Monceau**, on

Shell Beach

whose summit are more stones of early man. Even more existed before the quarrymen destroyed them. These monuments have been scientifically examined and their contents are in the Guernsey Museum in St Peter Port.

In early summer the common abounds with masses of burnet roses, dwarf flowers of immense appeal. They provide food for the multitude of rabbits which infest the island, despite frequent attacks of myxomatosis. Many other flowers grow in the sandy soil. Birds haunt the common and its curious, rather mysterious, character will at once impress the sensitive. Not for nothing did Mrs Compton Mackenzie write: 'At all costs propitiate the spirit of the island'.

Off the north-eastern corner of Herm is **Plat Houmet**, a flat islet abounding in sea fowl. Further away are masses of rocks and at low water some of them may be inspected, for a vast expanse of sand is then exposed. It is even possible to walk to **Vermerette beacon**, facing the harbour, where, some believe, traces of a Neolithic structure are to be seen at a low spring tide. This is one of the rocks marked by beacons and passed by the launches plying between Herm and Guernsey.

The sandy shores of northern Herm suffer from erosion in spite of the constant efforts to arrest it. So keep well away from the common's seaward edge, to prevent even more damage. Look at La Pierre aux Rats as you walk eastward and observe the profusion of islets lying northwards. They are **Les Amfrocques**, commonly named 'The Humps', and while at high tide they may seem rather unremarkable, at other times their considerable area and colourful characteristics can be seen to advantage.

At **La Pointe du Gentilhomme** (we shall never know his identity) the way leads south, along the flank of the Shell Beach, surely Herm's greatest attraction to the majority of its visitors. It is a rather straight expanse of shore line, in itself of no great beauty, but the millions of shell fragments (and sometimes whole shells) have been famous for many years, and countless specimens have been removed. In consequence, the Shell Beach is not quite what it used to be, yet it still encourages visitors to burrow in its depths in search of rarities. Peculiarities of tide and current are believed to have created this curious beach, which is good for bathing.

Belvoir House

Refreshments are available here and one can either turn inland and make for the harbour area or, better still, follow an enticing path southward. It runs along the base of gentle cliffs to **Belvoir Bay**, the most attractive inlet in the island. Its sands are very inviting and the clarity of the water is remarkable. One may eat and drink here, and watch the visiting yachts and the many folk who laze in the sun.

Herm's cliff paths are always in good condition but, even so, progress can be laborious to some, because the walk entails a certain amount of climbing up and down. Yet if one does this slowly the effort is not excessive, since the actual distance covered is relatively slight. There are resting-places, too, notably opposite the great crag of Caquorobert, accessible at low tide, after a scramble. Across the Great Russel lies Sark, and perhaps the French coast beyond it may be visible, as well as Jersey, away in the south-east.

The path runs southward, ascending and descending amid scenes of varied beauty. On the one hand there is the sea, presenting a picture of endless changes, on the other are the verdant slopes of

Herm's east coast. Below are small bays, inaccessible from the path, and high above are the borders of meadows, relatively large by Channel Islands' standards. The cliffs reach a maximum height of 190ft, but only become sheer near Le Creux Pignon, where a path runs inland to the farm road. Along this lies the so-called Deer Park, Herm's highest point, 203ft (62m) above sea level.

Le Creux was originally a cave with an aperture in its roof. This collapsed in 1964 and signs of erosion are still visible in this wild inlet. For this reason a stout barricade separates path from cliff edge. Before long the way goes down a flight of steps before reaching Herm's 'farthest south': Pointe Sauzebourge. It faces La Percée Passage and Jethou and here is an excellent pausing place with a good view.

The path, amid gorse bushes, winds northward and 100yd north of the headland an uncertain track, marked by some barbed wire fencing, leads up to the shaft of the copper mine, where so little of value was found. The mine is dangerous to explore and it is wiser to proceed to Rosière Cottage, the lower path, and the landing steps.

Looking seaward, beyond the landing, are two big reefs. At the southern extremity of the outer one is the so-called **Gate Rock**, visible to the keen eye when the launch passes it. The rock has a hole in it and tradition declares that here was once a field and the holed rock marked the site of a gate. It is far more likely to have held a boat mooring, possibly used when there was quarrying on nearby Crevichon, since the era of fields and gates was thousands of years later than the period when the present rock was part of the main island.

The beach at Belvoir Bay

Jethou

While Jethou is smaller than Herm (it is about 100 acres, or approximately 40ha, in area), it is higher; its cliffs rise to 268ft (about 100m). Its flat top is partly cultivated. On the north face is the Fairy Wood (so-called) and a large expanse of trees and scrub lies above the residence, on Jethou's west coast.

The house, once the home of Compton Mackenzie, dates from the eighteenth century, when John Allaire, a privateer, lived there. It has a most attractive garden, in which grows a splendid mulberry tree. Here may well have been the site where Restauld resided. In the eleventh century this worthy was shipmaster to Duke Robert of Normandy. Later the mariner became a monk and Jethou, given him by Robert, was donated to the Abbey of Mont St Michel. It passed into the possession of the Crown (its present owner) on the suppression of alien religious houses in 1416.

Subsequently, the island became the haunt of pirates and the

Jethou

The islands of Herm and Jethou at sunrise

Crown, endeavouring to discourage their activities, apprehended them and hanged them in chains on Jethou's summit as an example to others. In its time, like Herm, it was a hunting ground for Guernsey Governors and in the last century, during the building of St Peter Port's New Harbour, quarrying was carried out on Crevichon, the cone-shaped islet on the north. This, like La Grande Fauconnière, a more rugged stack on the south-east, is crowned by a whitewashed landmark. Both are accessible at low tide and abound in wildfowl, but are no longer open to visitors.

On Jethou's east coast is a very fine **creux** (a cave with a chimney), approached by a deep gully. Nearby is a raised beach, revealing a shore line high above the present level. The terraced hillside suggests bygone cultivation. Another possible relic of the past is a standing stone in the Fairy Wood, considered by some to be a menhir.

One of Jethou's tenants was Lieutenant-Colonel M. Fielden, who also rented Herm from the Crown. In 1867 the tenancy ended, when it was discovered that the colonel was using Jethou to store brandy which he was smuggling from France to England. The last tenant was Sir Charles Hayward, who died in 1983 and who made considerable improvements to the island.

──────── 2 ────────
ALDERNEY

With an area of approximately 6sq miles (1,554ha), this is the third largest of the Channel Islands and the most northerly. It is the closest to France, since the coast of Le Cotentin is a mere 9 miles away. Perhaps it is the least known of the group. Since World War II (when German troops were virtually its only inhabitants) it has emerged from its former obscurity, but it is still the least visited.

Yet Alderney was highly favoured (admittedly in a sombre fashion) by primitive man, as were its neighbours. Prehistoric burial structures were abundant until the last century, when most of them were destroyed by workmen engaged in turning the island into a fortress. But two survive: a cist near Fort Tourgis, on the north-west coast, and the remains of an Iron Age site on Longis Common, in the south-east. The cist's ancient name, Roc à l'Epine, suggests the former presence of a menhir there.

On the eminence known as Les Rochers, east of St Anne, are several stones scattered about, and, while many of these are of natural origin, archaeologists consider that ten of them are the remains of a dolmen. There is no certainty about their origin, however. The remains at Les Pourciaux, overlooking Longis Common, were so mutilated by the Germans that they are unrecognisable as dolmens, since they are now little more than a heap of stones.

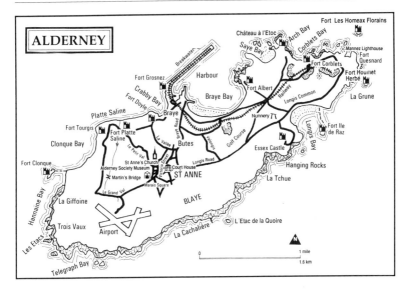

A considerable number of graves once existed on Longis Common, as well as on Raz Island, nearby. Others were located on the site of Chateau à l'Etoc, on the north coast. Roman remains suggest a Roman occupation of the island, especially in the Longis area. Coins have been found, chiefly of the second century AD, and it is considered likely that the so-called Nunnery, on the shores of Longis Bay, was built on Roman foundations. The archaeologist David Johnston is of the opinion that 'there was a substantial settlement of Roman date nearby', to quote from The *Channel Islands, an Archaeological Guide*.

Who brought Christianity to Alderney is not known. Doubtless it was introduced from Brittany, but the name of the missionary is obscure. A.H. Ewen, an authority on island history, dismisses the tradition that he was St Vignalis. Whoever he was, he did what others had done in the neighbouring islands, for several chapels were built near the sites of megaliths, as a counter-attack against their alleged evil influences. No trace of these buildings survives.

Written history begins in a Charter granted by Duke William (the future Conqueror) in 1042 to the Abbey of Mont St Michel, to which

Alderney was donated. Fifteen years later the island passed into the hands of the Bishop of Coutances, most of which he held for the following three centuries. The Crown, of course, was the official 'owner' of Alderney and in the reign of Henry VIII it was fortified with the aim of turning it into a naval base. The island's position as an outpost in the Channel and almost within sight of Cherbourg made it ideal for this purpose.

Despite the presence of feudalism in the other Channel Islands, no such system appears to have prevailed in Alderney. It was ruled by the King's Court, comprising six Jurats, magistrates as well as administrators, and a *Prevôt*, or Sheriff. The king owned a windmill, perhaps in competition with the bishop's watermill! The ancient function of open-field farming was practised on the Blaye, the high ground on the south coast, and traces of it survive. These strips of cultivated land adjoined the little town of St Anne, most of which, in medieval times, consisted of farmhouses. The Blaye covered about 450 acres (180ha) and very little other territory was under cultivation. Indeed, this is largely true today.

Alderney's harbour, such as it was, was at Longis and the remains of a pier are still visible on the western side of the bay. It was protected by the *Castrum Longini* (now the Nunnery) and by Essex Castle on the heights. Originally this was styled Les Murs de Haut and work on its construction began in 1546.

Operations ceased in 1554 and the building was only completed in Victorian times. The northern and western sides of the outer wall are Tudor. The name 'Essex' is associated with the Earl of Essex who, in 1591, bought the governorship of Alderney from John Chamberlain, who held it from the Crown. Essex, however, never seems to have lived on the island and, just prior to his execution for high treason, he leased Alderney to William Chamberlain (John's brother) and it remained in the hands of his family until 1643, by which time the castle was in ruins.

During the Civil War, the island was in the hands of a Parliamentary garrison, whose commander was Captain Nicholas Ling. He was the Lieutenant-Governor and also commanded the Alderney Militia, a post he held until 1679, when he died at the age of eighty. He built Government House, in St Anne's Square, now the Island Hall in renamed Connaught Square, and one of Alderney's finest buildings.

The Guernsey family of Le Mesurier became Hereditary Governors of Alderney through inheritance from Sir Edmond Andros (another Guernseyman), who had acquired the patent from the Jersey de Carterets. John Le Mesurier was unpopular in the island because of his Guernsey connections, but his son Henry proved more acceptable, thanks largely to his privateering enterprises, resulting in the building of a jetty at Braye in 1736. This became Alderney's harbour and the one at Longis was abandoned.

Henry's brother John succeeded him and it is on record that in 1779 his privateer *Resolution* brought in prizes valued at £134,589, a great fortune in those days. Privateering was a legal form of making vast sums of money in wartime. The king granted licences to privately-owned vessels to attack enemy shipping and such vessels and their cargoes reaped rich dividends, especially as war with France was more or less constant in the eighteenth century. Privateering and the export of Alderney cattle to England made the island a prosperous place, far removed from its earlier obscurity and consequent poverty.

Warehouses and dwellings were built at Braye — they still survive — and better houses lined the streets of St Anne, among them handsome Mouriaux House, just off Royal Connaught Square, built in 1779. Fortifications defended the coast, although not on the scale of those constructed in Victoria's reign, and the island became of importance strategically as well as commercially. Another improvement was the addition of a tower to the humble parish church, whose clock still tells the time in the High Street. The Governor endowed a school in 1790, not far from the Court House, built in 1770. Smuggling proved so profitable that it, too, transformed the face of Alderney.

John Wesley came to the island in 1787, preached at Braye and slept at the Divers Inn. As a result of his visit a Methodist chapel was built in 1790, to be succeeded by a better one in 1814.

In 1811, Telegraph Tower, on the western cliffs, was constructed above the bay of that name (formerly styled La Foulère). By means of a repeating signal at Le Mât, in Sark (near Beauregard Hotel) it was possible to communicate with Guernsey and Jersey, an invaluable advantage in wartime, when the approach of a French fleet could thus

The inner harbour, Alderney

be signalled in sufficient time to prepare for attack and invasion.

The ending of the Napoleonic Wars created poverty in Alderney and the ultimate suppression of smuggling worsened the situation. Privateers and free traders belonged to the past and the population declined in consequence. Matters were not improved when General John Le Mesurier surrendered his patent to the Crown and thus became the last hereditary Governor. The fashion of including Alderney cows in the herds of English country houses continued, although their export could have made little difference to the island's financial plight, which persisted for too many years.

Hereditary Governors did not solely govern the island, for administration was in the hands of a Judge (the first to be appointed was in 1612) and Jurats, and from this Court emerged the States of Alderney. The last Judge retired in 1949, when a new form of local government was inaugurated.

Whereas, after Waterloo, war between England and France became a thing of the past, the French were still regarded with some suspicion and when, in 1842, a breakwater and fortifications were built at Cherbourg, the British Government took swift action. It was resolved to create what was styled a harbour of refuge (more accurately a naval base) at Alderney and to fortify its coastline in strength. The island, so near Cherbourg, was considered to be 'The Key of the Channel' and the vast enterprise resulting from this belief transformed its appearance and way of life.

The naval port was at Braye and the mighty breakwater, so prominent a feature, was only a part of the scheme, for another harbour arm was planned, to run out from Roselle Point (below Fort Albert), although this was never completed. Hundreds of workmen were engaged to construct the mole and other defences and it was necessary to build houses to accommodate them at Newtown and elsewhere. A paddle steamer, the Queen of the Isles, was employed by the contractors to convey materials to the site and to provide a link with Guernsey. Interest in the work was so great that she also conveyed sightseers from that island to Braye. This must have been the birth of Alderney's tourist industry, for the visitors, having inspected the engineering marvels, discovered the excellence of the sandy bays, the majesty of the cliffs and, not least, the charm of St

PLACES OF INTEREST
IN ALDERNEY

Braye
Braye Street, Old Pier, New
(Crabby) Harbour, Breakwater,
Alderney sweater manufactory,
Crabby.

Forts (exterior)
Albert, Clonque, Essex Castle,
Houmet Herbe, Nunnery,
Quesnard, Raz Island.

German fortifications (exterior)
Tower at Mannez, anti-tank wall
at Longis and sundry bunkers,
also battery at Giffoine.

Railway
Garden at Bridge Martin (Little
Blaye).

St Anne
Church, Island Hall, Court
House, Museum, Town and
Butes, Pottery, Art Centre,
Cinema.

Note: *Early in August, Alderney
Week is held. It includes a
cavalcade, fancy dress parade,
torchlight procession, bonfire,
various competitions and sports.
It is the highlight of the season.*

Anne. As a result, Scott's Hotel was opened in Braye Road and other establishments followed at Braye and St Anne. A regular shipping service was established and Alderney became a popular resort (albeit on a small scale) for those in quest of peace and beauty. It has remained so ever since.

Local seafarers declared that Braye was no place for a breakwater, since it faced the might of heavy seas. They were right, for building work was often hindered by breaches in the mole, as a result of stormy weather and, to this day, the breakwater suffers grievously from time to time. Still, the work continued, regardless of expense. Part of the structure is submerged today (vessels give it a wide berth) and of its total length of 1,609yd only 967yd are visible. Before the breakwater was completed, the international situation had improved, and the Government had no use for it. Thought was given as to its demolition, but in the end it was retained and today the States of Guernsey maintain it as a part of a contribution to national defence.

Certainly it is imperative for the safety of Braye harbour but, argue the people of Alderney, it was not of their making. They did not ask for a breakwater, they do not own it and they could not afford its

Roadside war memorial, Alderney

upkeep. Today it is a boon to the angler and it forms an agreeable place in good weather. In adverse conditions it should be avoided, for great seas break over it in spectacular fashion. Its absence would result in their attacking Braye itself.

The chain of coastal forts was completed, despite the easing of tension, and they and the breakwater cost the Government £260,000, a great sum a century ago. Only Fort Albert was regularly used by the military, although Fort Essex (now Essex Castle) served as a garrison hospital, Fort Tourgis became a training place for the militia and Fort Grosnez is still occupied by the breakwater authorities. The States of Alderney own most of the forts, having bought them at a nominal price from the British Government, and the remainder are in private hands. These beautifully built strongholds, whose architecture incorporates some archaic features, add very materially to the character of the island, in sharp contrast with the more aggressive appearance of its German fortifications of alien concrete.

A cattle drinking fountain near Alderney's airport

August 21, 1850, was a great day for Alderney, for it was then that the excellent church of St Anne was consecrated by the Bishop of Winchester, of whose diocese the Channel Islands are a part. It was the gift of the Reverand John Le Mesurier, son of the last Governor, and it replaced the small and unworthy High Street edifice. The new church is large, for it was intended to accommodate both the Anglican population and the garrison. Methodists attend their church (dating from 1852) near Butes, the Roman Catholics used to worship at Crabby, until their church was desecrated during the Occupation, and the Salvation Army has its citadel in the High Street.

At the end of the last century a commercial jetty was built at Braye: It is far superior to the ancient Douglas Quay and to the picturesque Little Crabby Harbour (also called the New Harbour), which dries out at low tide. It was constructed during the building of the breakwater for ships engaged in the construction work. In the roadstead many yachts cast anchor and the scene in summer is a lively one.

World War I made comparatively little impact on Alderney.

Certainly it was garrisoned, but then this was customary, although greater vigilance against possible enemy action was maintained. Quarrying, an important industry begun when stone was needed for breakwater and forts, continued, but cattle exports diminished.

The conflict over, the island settled down to its normal, peaceful way of life, a quality not really disturbed when, in 1935, one of the first Channel Islands airports was built on the Blaye. It was, in truth, but a landing strip and was an improvement on the days when aircraft used the sands of Braye. Today's airport is much bigger and better. Few used the original one in the 1930s, for the vast majority of visitors, islanders and troops travelled in the staunch little steamer *Courier*, which plied between Guernsey and Alderney for a great many years, regardless of turbulent seas and, between 1914 and 1918, of the possibility of encountering hostile submarines in the Channel.

For the first 9 months of World War II Alderney, like its neighbours, was placid enough. Some troops were sent there for training and, as time went on, their numbers increased, but they scarcely disturbed the islanders, who were glad of their presence, nevertheless. The population then numbered about 1,400. It was not until early in June 1940, that clouds appeared on the horizon, for the Germans, sweeping all before them, had reached Cherbourg and from its peninsula the first island they beheld was Alderney.

At this period its sister-isles were perturbed at this turn of affairs and numbers of young folk, especially schoolchildren, were evacuated. Yet the majority of the inhabitants remained, despite ever-mounting fears of invasion. The people of Alderney were not kept informed of the military situation, unlike their neighbours, and when its garrison was withdrawn consternation increased and bewilderment prevailed.

Undoubtedly, the proximity of Alderney to the French coast induced practically all its people to forsake its shores. A few did so on their own initiative, but the bulk of them, under the guidance of Judge J.G. French, resolved to leave *en masse*, only a handful of people electing to stay. The dramatic account of this poignant chapter in the island's history is well told in *The Alderney Story*, by M. St J. Packe and M. Dreyfus. For the story of how the island fared during its occupation by the Germans, consult *Alderney, Fortress Island*, by T.X.H. Pantcheff.

It was on 2 July that a small number of troops crossed from Guernsey to take possession of Alderney. Unlike the other islands, it was almost deserted, for only seven civilians were there to meet them. Their motives for remaining is a matter of speculation, but later they were joined by a force of Guernseymen, sent there to assist in farm work and especially in harvesting. Their stay, however, was relatively brief, although a good deal of land was cultivated, especially on the Blaye.

It was in October 1941, that Alderney was transformed into a fortress. Jersey and Guernsey received similar treatment, but with a difference, since they had considerably larger populations, in contrast with deserted Alderney, and this gave the Germans greater scope in their exploitation of the island. Hundreds of slave workers were imported from Europe to build great concrete fortifications. They were treated vilely and, since civilian witnesses were absent, it appears that their sufferings were even harsher than those in the larger islands.

St Anne's Church was desecrated, dwellings were violated or destroyed, land boundaries were uprooted. A pier was built at Braye, forming an extension to the jetty, the railway, used in the construction of the breakwater and in its maintenance, was employed in the carriage of building materials. The wretched workers lived in disgraceful conditions in camps, the garrison was increased and the face of Alderney was mutilated.

Thousands of mines were laid around the shores, a great anti-tank wall arose at Longis Bay and, close by, a mighty tower was built. A massive battery covered the Swinge (the channel separating Alderney from Burhou) and bunkers appeared everywhere. The old forts were re-fortified, barbed wire festooned the beaches, underwater obstacles, aircraft deterrents and booms across some of the bays were features of fortified Alderney. At Les Mouriaux, in the town, arose a gaunt concrete tower; there was a cemetery for slaveworkers at Longis, and another, for Germans, on the Longis Road.

The RAF was not ignorant of these developments, neither was the Royal Navy unaware of this menace in the Channel and in 1942 the battleship *Rodney* shelled a battery from 20 miles away. British troops made a reconnaissance landing on Les Casquets lighthouse and took prisoner the Germans occupying it. This was also in 1942, the year in which a small raid was carried out on Burhou.

The end of this depressing period came on 16 May 1945, when British troops took possession of the island after its German garrison had surrendered. It was hardly a 'liberation', since only a small party of civilians were present and they were full of stories of German brutality towards the slave-workers. In due course work began on the island's rehabilitation, a most formidable task, since its defences, mines and impedimenta were legion, many of its buildings were in ruins or in a deplorable condition; immense restoration work was inevitable and the prospect was so daunting that the British Government, faced with this task, seriously considered abandoning Alderney and leaving it to its fate.

Happily, this did not transpire. It was months before the exiles could return home and when they did so they were appalled at what they saw. But they were undaunted and, with substantial aid from Britain and Guernsey, the great work of recovery was undertaken. It was a worthwhile job and, while the operation took years, the result was an Alderney almost as fair as it used to be.

In 1949 the island was given a new constitution, with the head of affairs changing from a Judge to a President of the States. Formerly the Judge presided over both Court and States. The innovation decreed that the Court should have a Jurat as chairman and that its members should have no hand in insular government. Both bodies meet in the same building, however. Changes were made in taxation, education and social services, making Alderney more dependent on Guernsey than previously. In compensation, two Alderney representatives attend Guernsey States Meetings.

Post-war developments include an excellent airport, a new school, a fine hospital, a library and a museum. A great many new houses have been built, some of them less decorative than others. Road surfaces, on the whole, are good, motor vehicles are far more numerous than in pre-war days. There have been royal visits in post-war decades (including two by the Queen) and very welcome have been those of the submarine *Alderney* and, later, of the fishery

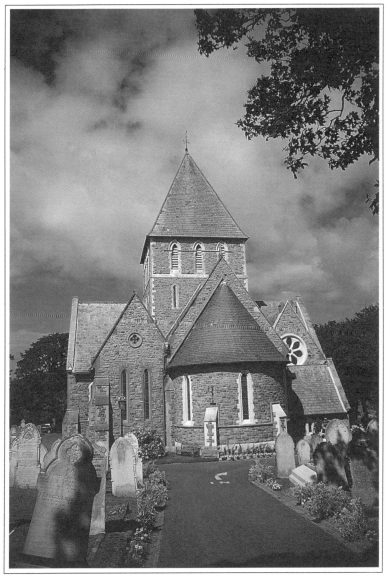

St Anne's Church

protection ship also named after the isle of her adoption.

The 'capital' of Alderney, **St Anne**, is, in fact, its only town, in which the bulk of the population resides. There are clusters of dwellings at Braye and Newtown, with scattered buildings elsewhere, but St Anne is by far the most important concentration, the island's hub and heart. Here are its places of worship, the majority of hotels, the administration and commercial centres, and what was once a collection of farmhouses has become one of the most fascinating towns in the Channel Islands, even if it is one of the smallest. To style it a village would be inaccurate and yet, in some aspects, it resembles one.

To savour its atmosphere and to study its architectural features, one must stroll through the streets, most of which fortunately retain their paving stones. As good a place as any from which to begin this perambulation is **Butes**, the 'village green', a grassy expanse used partly for sporting activities and also as a strolling place from which magnificent views can be enjoyed. 'Butes' signifies an archery ground on which, no doubt, early militiamen exercised their bows.

The outlook embraces Braye harbour and bay, Burhou, Ortac and Les Casquets, much of eastern Alderney and a vast distance seaward, obviously depending on visibility. Passing ships are often numerous and the arrival and departure of local callers are well seen from Butes, from which a serpentine path winds downhill to Braye. It passes through rather rough terrain, in which gorse and blackberry bushes abound. Adjoining the greensward are Belle Vue Hotel and what remains of Grand Island Hotel, burnt to the ground in 1981. One may still use some of its amenities, including the swimming pool. Nearby are the former militia gun sheds, now States workshops.

 Butes, on the south, adjoins the foot of Victoria Street, St Anne's main thoroughfare, and to reach it pass the Methodist Church, a well-designed building of 1852. On either side of the street are relatively small shops, nearly all of which have a character far removed from the supermarket and multiple store. Some are elegant, all have friendly staffs, and to shop in Alderney is a joy. Before Queen Victoria's visit the street's name was Rue Grosnez, because it led to a part of Braye so called. Halfway up is the Albert Memorial, also recalling Alderney's first royal visit, and this handsome arch graces the main approach to **St Anne's Church**.

This is probably the finest modern church in the Channel Isles, designed by Sir Giles Gilbert Scott. It is spacious, excellently built of warm, ruddy Alderney stone and its handsome tower is a landmark, even though the church stands in a hollow. Had its site been more elevated it would have been still more impressive. Before entering it, spare a glance at some of the tombs in its well-kept churchyard.

The interior of St Anne's Church is most dignified, and its proportions are admirable. When it was filled with troops and civilians it must have been a fine sight, and even today, on great occasions, its pews are full. Before the German Occupation the building was noteworthy. It suffered degradation by the enemy, but has been superbly restored. The windows (chiefly modern) deserve close scrutiny and notice especially the lovely window at the east end, the altars and, at the western extremity, the Le Mesurier memorials in brass. The bells are splendid and to hear them ring out is one of the delights of Alderney. How fortunate that they were recovered from the Germans just in time, for they had been removed to Cherbourg for melting down.

Near the churchyard, by the south gate, running up to Queen Elizabeth II Street (formerly New Street and originally Rue des Héritiers) is the **Court House**, built in 1850. Here sit the Court and, at other times, the States, and their meetings are worth attending. The assembly chamber has been restored (after misuse in the Occupation) in excellent taste. On one wall is a valuable painting of General John Le Mesurier surrendering his patent to the Crown. It once hung at Mouriaux House, the Le Mesurier family home, and was painted by John Linnell. In 1981 the Alderney States acquired the picture for £22,000. To visit the Court chamber, first apply at the enquiry office downstairs.

Within the Court House are sundry exhibits of historical interest. It also accommodates Court and States offices. The police station and gaol adjoin the Court House. Eastwards Victoria Street is rejoined at a point a little above the War Memorial garden. Close by is the Post Office and the Albert Inn.

Further up Victoria Street is Ollivier Street on the left and, nearly opposite this turning, is the Chez André Hotel. Across the road is the

Art Centre and a little way down the street is the Georgian House Hotel. The way upward soon joins High Street, once the town's main thoroughfare, but now secondary to Victoria Street. Turning left is the Jubilee Home for the elderly and on the other side of the road is the Salvation Army citadel. Several High Street houses are attractive: so are the buildings in Le Bourgage, an old street running south of High Street, nearly opposite the Campania pub.

Off Le Bourgage is La Brecque, leading to the Blaye. The western end of Le Bourgage joins La Venelle de Simon, a rugged, narrow lane which leads to Le Huret, near the clock tower. Turn left and in a few yards is Marais Square, where once cattle drank at its fountain. Today it is the bus terminus and, on New Year's Day, it is where the fire brigade traditionally practise, turning the hoses on all who venture too near! The Marais Hotel stands here, near Little Street (another attractive approach to the Blaye) and adjoining a series of delightful lanes leading to **Royal Connaught Square**.

Until the Duke of Connaught visited Alderney in 1905, this was known as St Anne's Square. Here stands the vicarage and, opposite, the Royal Connaught Hotel. The most impressive building there is the Island Hall, once Government House and later a convent. It was built in 1763 and is now States property. It houses the excellent Alderney Library and its hall is used for dramatic performances, concerts, public meetings and other functions. Its Anne French Room has often been the scene for royal receptions.

Just off the square (past the hotel) is **Mouriaux House**, a stately residence and possibly the best private dwelling in the island. Unhappily, an ugly German tower confronts it. Beyond the house one may reach the airport or descend to the north coast. The way to the Alderney Pottery is nearby. But as the town ramble is not yet completed leave the square at the vicarage end and walk up the incline to Le Huret where, in olden times, the island Court met in the open air. This is one of the places where official proclamations are still made. Not far away is the Rose and Crown Hotel.

The **Alderney Society's museum** is most certainly worth viewing. Its neighbour is the clock tower, sole remnant of the ancient parish church, whose adjacent graveyard is worth a brief visit. The museum, once the island's school, houses an archaeological collec-

Island Hall

tion of importance, many German Occupation relics, nautical exhibits, pictures and photographs. The building dates from 1790, as an
inscription, in French, over the entrance testifies.

Continuing along High Street eastward, reach the Coronation pub
and the top of Victoria Street. Saunter down its pleasant shop-lined
pavements to Ollivier Street. This leads to Le Val, a hill running from
the top of Braye Road to High Street and forming something of a town
bypass. Walk down Le Val, passing the States Dairy, to Les
Rocquettes, close to which is the Roman Catholic Church of St Anne
and St Mary Magdalen. It was completed in 1958 and replaces the
former church at Crabby which the Germans spoilt. The new one,
viewed from within, is admirable.

At the foot of Victoria Street a steep, cobbled lane runs down to
the Terrace, a public garden pleasantly wooded. Across the road, Le
Pré, is St Anne's Church. From the Terrace a most attractive road,
'The Valley', leads down to Saline Bay and Crabby. It is one of the
approaches to Alderney's north coast and the port of Braye.

From St Anne to Braye the distance is approximately three quarters of a mile (1 1/2 km) and from Braye to Longis, via Mannez, about 2 1/2 miles (5km).

The easiest way down to **Braye Harbour** is via the main road from St Anne's, used by buses and much other traffic. Agreeable enough, but more attractive, if a little rougher, is the serpentine path from Butes. It pursues its course through undeveloped country and in its lower reaches are paths running left, right and centre, all ending at or near Braye. Rejoin the main road where a path (right) leads to the turning to Newtown (where stands Harbour Lights Hotel) and follow Braye Road to Braye Gates, where the diminutive Alderney railway station is to be found.

Small trains travel to Mannez quarry and the ride is very enjoyable, indeed, it is much too brief: there are unusual views of the island. Alderney is fortunate in having retained its railway, which Jersey and Guernsey have lost. The Alderney Railway Society opened the service in 1980 with an electric locomotive, acquiring a steam one in 1982. Enthusiastic amateurs man both trains and station.

Braye Street is full of character. On the one hand is the row of eighteenth-century houses, whose backs are practically on Braye beach and which include the Divers Inn and its neighbour, the Sea View Hotel. On the other side are old warehouses and yards. Places of refreshment are not wanting, and most enjoy extensive views over coast and harbour. The Sailing Club's headquarters adjoin the harbourmaster's office, below which a road leads to Little Crabby (or New) Harbour, best seen when the tide is full. Ancient cannon serve as bollards and are believed to have come from HMS *Amethyst*, which sank in the Swinge in 1796.

The commercial quay dates from the start of the present century and here berth cargo vessels and the occasional warship. Sometimes yachts, French fishing boats and Trinity House ships use the quay, at whose extremity the Germans built an extension. This fell into dangerous decay and it was demolished in 1981. Much more ancient is the Old Jetty and Douglas Quay, seldom used by ships nowadays, though swimmers and sunbathers enjoy their mellow granite and massive shelter. A small lighthouse at the end of the pier flashes in conjunction with another near Braye Gates. The old harbour has the disadvantage of drying out at low tide hence the building of the newer one, which lacks the character of the older haven.

Braye sands form an ideal bathing place and also an enjoyable walk to the Fort Albert area. Equally fine is a stroll along Le Banquage, a grass strip bordering the bay and, on the other side of the road, the railway line. And, if walking is to your liking, try the breakwater — but choose a calm day!

The East End of Alderney

The walk eastward from Braye along its sands, greensward or road, is good. Seaward, there is always something to observe and the inland scene is not without interest, with its golf course to see and, perhaps, for later use. Ahead looms **Fort Albert**, on Mont Touraille, the master fort of Alderney. Today it is derelict and closed to the public and its owners, the States, have yet to decide its destiny. At its feet are Mount Hale Battery, the Arsenal (now comprising flats and otoros) and the former garrison football pitch. An unusual covered way, in granite, runs from the Arsenal to the fort's entrance.

A somewhat rough road extends from the Whitegates houses at the crossroads to the fort's gate and it continues to a point overlooking Braye and the harbour approaches. Below is Roselle Battery, where searchlights were once mounted. The environs of Fort Albert bear pronounced evidence of the Occupation, the site having been heavily fortified by the Germans. Today it all looks rather desolate, a far cry from the time when, with a British garrison in residence, Fort Albert was immaculate.

An agreeable path runs downhill to the rugged headland of Bibette and to Saye Bay, with its inviting sands and islet. Here the troops used to bathe. Dunes flank the landward side, where there is Alderney's official camp site, at Saye farm. In a commanding position stands Château à l'Etoc, on the eastern side of the bay. Behind it is Hermitage Battery, standing near the site of the original *château*, for the present building is largely Victorian, with a dash of German work, too! Its neighbour is Arch Bay, so named because of a tunnel running

Braye Bay

Alderney railway

under the road leading to the fort. Formerly it was used by carts collecting *vraic* from the shore and it aided them to pass from Saye to the fine sands of **Corblets Bay**.

To many, this is Alderney's best bay. It is easy of access (buses stop there), the surf is usually excellent and appears fairly frequently, it is safe and the rocks, if uncomfortable as seats (for the strata is up-tilted), are at least interesting to examine. Dominating the scene is **Fort Corblets**, a very handsome and most comfortable residence. Despite its elegance, it still retains a martial air and happily traces of German additions are barely evident. This is, in truth, a most attractive corner of Alderney. The road winds around the fort's gardens and passes an extraordinary-looking rocky pinnacle. Rugged grandeur is on the left and on the opposite side are quarries, one of which, at Mannez, yields stone for breakwater maintenance and its yard is the railway terminus. Above the quarry stands a massive German tower.

Mannez lighthouse, looming ahead, is handsome and in normal

Fort Corblets

conditions it may be visited in the afternoon. The view from its lantern is vast. At night, its beams are visible from several parts of the island and in fog its powerful siren joins that of Les Casquets in dismal warning. Fort Les Hommeaux Florains, the lighthouse's neighbour, is ruined and can only be reached by a rock climb and a brief swim. It is easier to visit Fort Quèsnard, just past the lighthouse, although it is perhaps one of the least exciting of Alderney's forts.

While the main road, proceeds inland until it reaches the shores of Longis, the walker is best advised to use the coastal path. It is one of Alderney's best walks, with its wild, rocky coastline, comfortable-looking dwellings inland, the delightful Fort Houmet Herbé (accessible at low tide) and, beyond the Race, the fair face of France. Off the fort is the Brinchetais reef, a danger to the mariner and an impressive sight to the landsman. Various gullies are good for bathing when tidal conditions permit.

The path runs parallel with the road at the eastern end of spacious **Longis Bay**, another favourite with visitors and islanders. Its sands

Corblets Bay and Mannez lighthouse

are broad and the great German anti-tank wall provides shelter to the sunbather. A causeway runs out to Raz Island and is only covered at high tide. A visit to Raz is recommended. Its defences, old and new, can be inspected. There is also an art gallery as well as a collection of stuffed birds. To stand on the battlements and survey the prospect over land and sea is a gratifying experience.

At the other end of Longis Bay is the Nunnery, the ancient fort, probably Roman in origin, which earned its name (so it is believed) because its garrison found it so lonely! The Germans made use of it and today it is a private residence. On the beach below the building are remains of an ancient wall, which has fallen onto the sands. Inland is Longis Common, rather desolate. There are traces of quarrying, a few houses and the remains of German defences. Here, long ago, dwelt the folk of Alderney, whose dead were buried in this forsaken place. It may well be that others of more exalted rank were also laid to rest at Longis. Unhappily, these remains have been destroyed by industry and invaders.

However, one important piece of prehistory survives: the **Iron Age site**, discovered in 1968 during the laying out of the golf course. Opposite the Nunnery is a road running northward and a few yards along it a sign points to the site. There is not a great deal to see, but the pots discovered may be viewed at the museum. It is believed that the site was once a workshop where pottery was made. Across the road is the residence named The Kennels and here, in 1972, the remains of a supposed Roman building were unearthed.

From the Nunnery one may return to St Anne by several ways. The route goes to Braye via Whitegates (passing the former coastguards' cottages) and then climbs the hill to the town. A cliff path skirting Essex Castle is recommended, or one may use Essex Glen, whose inconspicuous entrance is nearly opposite the Barn restaurant. The glen is pretty, though sometimes damp underfoot, and ultimately it joins the Longis Road near Devereux House Hotel. From there the way westward to St Anne is unmistakeable, if a little dull.

Longis Bay from Essex Castle

Alderney's High Lands

Braye to Clonque $1^1/_2$ miles (3km); Clonque to Longis (via cliffs) approximately 3 miles (6km).

The island's high ground comprises more than half its total area and, for most of its coastal perimeter, excellent cliff paths aid the walker. For some of the way, the motorist is catered for, but unless one is prepared to proceed on foot, the beauty and character of these highlands cannot be appreciated to the full. One may reach the cliffs from St Anne by several routes over the Blaye, that large, partly cultivated region bordering the south coast, but another approach is via the north coast, reached from the valley.

Heavy seas often pound the sands of **Saline Bay** and the swimmer there must be strong and prudent. Perhaps it is better to stride over the beach than to plunge into that crystal, tempting water, which could prove hazardous. In the bay's centre is **Fort Platte**

Saline, now used by a company which excavates and exports much beach material from an apparently endless source. The Swinge and Burhou lie seaward and further off are gannet-haunted Ortac, with its snowy cap, and the remote, aloof Casquets rocks. The scene is splendid — always.

The coast road leads to the outliers of Fort Tourgis and continues past its outer walls. This road may be followed to **Fort Clonque**, or by following Le Petit Val road up the hill the fort may be seen at close quarters. It is worthy of examination. A short distance beyond its entrance, just off the road on its seaward side, is the Tourgis dolmen. A track close by runs downhill and joins the coastal road by Clonque Cottage. The beach is a rocky one, ideal for the scrambler and for exploring the rock pools. Fort Clonque is conspicuous at the bay's extremity and it can be reached (other than at high tide) by a causeway. Hannaine Bay, suitable for bathing when its sand is exposed, lies in the shelter of this picturesque fort, owned by the Landmark Trust. From the fort the way lies uphill and the route is by a zigzag path, often decorated with banks of heather and alive with gorse. The grassy track continues through fields past a small brick building and, for a while, a stretch of road must be followed, running in a south-westerly direction, ie, one turns right, not using the route leading back to St Anne. Alderney, unfortunately, has very few signposts.

Take the second turning on the right which is a rough path running to the heights of **La Giffoine**, once the site of a beacon (for use in time of war) and, of more recent date, where massive German defence works stand. Below them a path runs part of the way down the cliffs and from here there is a close view of the multitude of gannets on the Garden Rocks.

Nearby, on the left, is the region of Trois Vaux: three shallow, treeless valleys converging at a cliff-edge from which access to the bay is difficult. The climb back to the road is rather tiring and it is tempting to take the distant prospect of Trois Vaux 'as read'. There is no precise cliff path between La Giffoine and Telegraph Bay, so return to the road until a right-hand turning leads to the top of the path and steps leading to Telegraph Bay. Its grandeur can be appreciated from the headlands at its extremities, but only from the beach can one

MILK-A-PUNCH SUNDAY

A pleasing custom peculiar to Alderney is that observed on the first Sunday in May. Pubs then offer customers an appetising free drink, limited to one glass per person, and comprising rum punch made to recipes peculiar to each establishment. The custom is said to have originated from the days when islanders took to the pastures, milked the nearest cow (without leave) and added rum and sugar to the yield. Why this had to be done on that particular Sunday is a mystery, though it may well hark back to the ancient May Day festival, still observed in Cornwall and elsewhere. In Alderney, the really enterprising strive to visit as many pubs (and hotels) as possible, not only to enjoy the maximum amount of liquor, but to compare one blend with another.

truly realise the scale of its great cliffs and the height of the tremendous rocks, La Nache and La Fourquie, which dominate the sands.

The way down is by no means difficult (though the return is rather hard going), but always consider the state of the tide before visiting **Telegraph Bay**; on a rising tide, the base of the cliff path may be inaccessible from the beach. The remains of the telegraph cable and a fine cave are seen at sea level, while the beautiful colours in the rocks and shingle are worthy of scrutiny, like the rock pools. Bathing is excellent there, and comparative solitude can be relied upon.

On regaining the cliff path (wide enough for vehicles in places) the walker will observe a track running to Telegraph Tower, a sturdy building, closed to the public, but from the cliff edge (where a German look-out post lurks) another extensive view is to be enjoyed. In clear weather all the other Channel Islands are visible, the glasshouses of Guernsey often glinting in the sunlight.

The coastal route forsakes its name temporarily when it proceeds inland for some distance, although in places one may, with a scramble, reach the cliff edge. Valleys descend to sea level, but no path accompanies their streams to the beach. The walker may rest on several seats along the way, whose landward side is flanked by the airport. At times, aircraft may disturb one's rest as they take off or land. Ahead stands a large, modern house on the cliffs and soon after the track runs closer to their edge.

Just before the way continues above the rock mass of L'Etac de la Quoire, offshore, a rather faint trail runs down the cliff to the ruined pier and stone-works of **La Cachalière**. The place is of some interest, though it is also rather desolate and probably those who visit it most are anglers. Alderney's cliffs are steep and lofty and, to be frank, they only really justify climbing at Telegraph Bay. Anglers and a few others, especially naturalists, frequent Bluestone Beach, access to which, at low tide, is by way of a scramble from the abandoned quarry at La Cachalière. Once again, the tide must be watched carefully.

Eastward the cliff path continues, with the Blaye as its neighbour, and tracks across its acres return to St Anne, not far off. The hardy walker, however, will elect to march on, passing the cliffs at La Haize with distaste, since it is here that the island's rubbish is dumped. Conditions improve above the inlet of the curiously named La Tchue and the path begins to ascend the heights on which Essex Castle stands.

German fortifications abound here, and below them, halfway down the slope, are the **Hanging Rocks**, one greater than the other. Both lean over like the Tower of Pisa and the legend is that, once upon a time, Jerseymen, anxious to acquire Alderney, secured a rope from one of these rocks to their boat, in an endeavour to tow the island away. All they did was to tilt the rock!

Soon the path becomes a road and skirts the castle, outside which yet another wide-ranging view unfolds and a descent to Longis. The return to St Anne could be made by bus or, if walking is still an attraction, by the Longis Road.

Little effort is required to walk to the beauty spot of **Martin's Bridge** and the reward is generous. Leave St Anne from the Royal Connaught Square, pass Les Mouriaux House (with the ghastly German tower opposite) and pursue a field track running west past modern houses. It traverses the Little Blaye and, after a while, the way becomes indistinct. Carry on westward, nevertheless, and a copse ahead marks a concealed path. It leads to a so-called bridge (more properly an embankment) crossing a shallow valley, down which runs a stream to Watermill Farm, below Fort Tourgis. Adjoining

this agreeable stone 'bridge' is a beautiful garden, a most unex-

Gannets on the Garden Rocks

Trois Vaux Bay

pected delight in such a place. Just over the 'bridge' is a path on the right, traversing Le Val de la Bonne Terre and terminating at a derelict water mill. If one ignores this turning, the path leads to the main road running from Fort Tourgis to Rose Farm, the large property near the airport. The return to St Anne could be via this route, and the whole walk covers but a mile or so.

BY SEA AROUND ALDERNEY

A marine tour of Alderney's shores is not to be missed. If possible, arrange a trip with a boatman at the New Harbour when you will pass the yachts and other craft moored in the lee of the great breakwater. The course may be eastward or westward, according to the tide. If the course is towards the west on rounding the breakwater, one enters the Swinge channel.

The boat heads for Burhou and soon birds form the escort: lordly gannets, screaming gulls, flitting oyster-catchers and, as the boat approaches Burhou, puffins fly all around. There was a time when they were far more numerous than they are now, but those remaining are most fascinating to observe, with their multi-coloured beaks and comical expression. The boat pauses offshore to watch the birds and to study Burhou's rugged coast at close quarters.

On the north coast of Alderney the heights are gentle and on the slope west of Braye the shape of Fort Tourgis is barely seen, so well does it blend with the landscape. A sterner picture is presented above Clonque, whose fort, again, merges into the scene so effectively.

As the boat draws near to the Garden Rocks (more accurately **Les Etacs** — the stacks) there is an astounding sight. Hundreds of gannets are perched on the massive crags, often nesting in close proximity with each other. The majesty of the rocks (which the boat approaches very closely) and the splendour of its occupants form an unforgettable sight. The gannets settled off Alderney (at Les Etacs and Ortac, near Les Casquets) in 1940 and have returned there each spring ever since.

To stand on the Alderney cliffs is to enjoy some excellent views, but to be at their feet is the only way to truly appreciate their majesty. Boat trips usually proceed to within a stone's throw of tremendous crags, natural arches, numerous caverns and green slopes rising to the cliff summits. From the coastal path one can have little idea of what lies below, as a descent of the sheer cliffs, save in one or two places, is impossible.

The boat passes Trois Vaux (whose three shallow valleys are visible above a forsaken beach) and then, wedged in the rocks, are the trivial remains of the small oil tanker *Point Law*, wrecked there in 1975. Telegraph Bay is entered and, if the tide is low, its sands will be visible. The path down is barely noticeable from the sea, but the caves and enormous rocks amaze the observer.

Alderney's geology can be studied closely, if rather briefly, from the boat and its contorted strata and attractive bands in the rock faces compose a wonderful prospect. So do the gullies, isolated rocks, clear sea and soaring water fowl. Less lovely, but still of interest, are the ruins of Cachaliere pier, where stone was once quarried and shipped. Offshore is **L'Etac de la Quoire**, an isolated stack like Cocq Lihou, west of it.

Bluestone Beach has a shingle shore, unlike most other Alderney bays. While it may be reached at low tide after a precarious scramble, it is scarcely worth the effort and the tide must not be forgotten. It is preferable to view it from the comfort of the boat, which heads eastward towards the bulky Hanging Rocks. They stand on the slope below Essex Castle, whose lower defences are Frying Pan Battery and Longis Lines, seen from the *Beverley Rose* as she approaches Longis Bay.

Below these defences are fretted rocks, contrasting with the bay's broad sands. At its eastern end stands Raz Island, whose fort is well seen as the boat passes by, giving the troubled Brinchetais reef a wide berth. **Fort Houmet Herbé**'s mellow stone looks pleasing, and to the right the shores of France are easily visible when the day is clear. The boat enters rather troubled waters at the confluence of the Alderney Race and the Swinge, but after Mannez lighthouse conditions are calmer.

At Corblets Bay, the fort may be admired and the lofty and less pleasing German tower inland noticed. Past Château à l'Etoc is the agreeable bay of Saye and then the rocks, gullies and cliffs of Mont Touraille, whose crown is Fort Albert. After crossing Braye Bay the breakwater slip is reached after a 2-hour marine excursion which must rank as one of the best in the Channel Isles.

Burhou island is about half a mile in length and 250ft (76m) wide. It is low-lying and its highest point is less than 40ft (12m) above the Swinge, the channel separating the island from Alderney. It has magnificent rock masses, both inland and around its wild coastline, and those who land there may well feel that they are on a desert island, for the cottage and hut do very little to lessen the impression of sublime desolation which Burhou produces on the sensitive visitor.

Much of its plant life comprises sea spurry and its friable soil has been greatly undermined by rabbit burrows and puffins' nests, resulting in a crumbling effect. To tread warily is provident, therefore. Visitors, however, are comparatively rare, since the *Beverley Rose* only infrequently stops at Burhou long enough for a landing. Nevertheless, she will take those wishing to stay there, taking their own provisions and drinking water. Permission to stay must first be obtained from the States Office, in Queen Elizabeth II Street. Enquiries about the sea trip should be made at Braye (☎ Alderney 2375).

Before the last war a stone cottage stood in the centre of Burhou and there was a time when a little farming was carried out by a French couple residing there. The building was available for bird-watchers and others wishing to spend a while on the island and it was also a place of refuge for shipwrecked sailors. The cottage was shattered by the Germans, whose gunners on La Giffoine used it for target practice. After the war a hut was set up in its ruins, but today the cottage has been rebuilt. Nearby is an observation 'hide'.

Little Burhou, on the western side, is separated from the rest of the island at high water and a racing tide runs between them. Beyond Little Burhou is a great reef and north of it is another, Le Renonquet, on which the destroyer *Viper* was stranded in fog during naval manoeuvres in 1901. She was by no means the first vessel to be lost off Burhou. Oddly enough, the vegetation of Little Burhou is completely different from its bigger neighbour. The island is, then, of much interest to the botanist, as well as to the ornithologist, the geologist and the lover of solitude.

Between Burhou and Les Casquets stands **Ortac**, a great stack, 79ft (24m) above sea level and the haunt of gannets since 1940. It is possible that boatmen at Braye will agree to take visitors there and if this is so, a great experience will be enjoyed. Like the Garden Rocks, Ortac is easily climbed by the agile and soon one is among the gannets, whose nests are scarcely fragrant! The great birds tolerate human beings, but they should be treated with caution.

On one of the rocks of **Les Casquets** stands a powerful lighthouse. A beacon has shone its warning to mariners since 1785, when a coal fire was burned there. Soon afterwards three lighthouses were built and their towers remain. One houses the present powerful light (of 2,850,000 candle power), whose visibility is 17 miles (27km), another accommodates the charging plant for a radio beacon and lighting, while in the third is a powerful fog signal.

Les Casquets lighthouse is about 9 miles (14km) from Alderney and during the Occupation a raiding party from England captured the Germans who manned it. Off Les Casquets foundered HMS *Victory* in 1744, with the loss of 1,000 lives and in 1899 the mail packet *Stella* struck the rocks in fog and sank, taking 102 of those aboard with her. The lighthouse is not open to the public.

3
SARK

O f all the Channel Islands, Sark is regarded with the greatest affection by most visitors. Even its history has an air of romance about it which its neighbours lack. If Alderney, in the past, was styled 'The Key of the Channel', Sark was its 'Gem'. Unquestionably, it has a coastline second to none in the islands and, while some of its erstwhile interior beauty has rubbed off in the march of Time, the element of charm prevails strongly. It is feudal, it almost lacks motor traffic and aircraft are banned. All these merits are not to be disputed and the wonder is (as with Herm) that the heavy tread of popularity has not done more damage than is the case.

Communications in summer are excellent. There is a frequent service of fast and comfortable launches (well protected from the elements) running from St Peter Port, together with a larger vessel, carrying cargo. To go there for a few hours is delightful, but to stay longer is even better. A day visit affords a sample of Sark's appeal, a week or more provides the full repast. Hotels and guest-houses are plentiful and to be in Sark after the day visitors have departed (and on Sundays, when no excursions are run) is to savour a sense of peace which surpasses anything of the kind found elsewhere. A day visit, if one wishes to see anything of the island, is necessarily something of a rush; a longer one permits a closer inspection, a

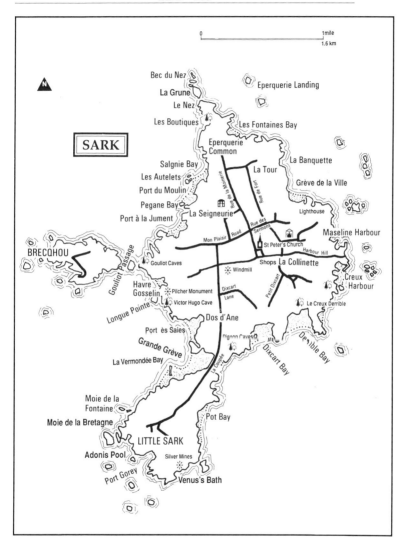

leisurely stay and the opportunity of embarking on a memorable boat tour which a shorter call cannot include. In short, Sark is worth more than a day.

Two of the most popular forms of transport on car-free Sark

Unlike the other Channel Isles, Sark's prehistoric remains are few, although perhaps they were once more numerous. They are confined to Little Sark, where there are two cists (small burial chambers), both on private property. One lies on the cliffside between Port Gorey and Venus Pool, the other, less visible, is on the estate of La Vermondaye, just over La Coupée. The relative lack of megaliths may be due to the height and steepness of Sark's cliffs. Its coastline is uniformly high, discouraging landing and the building of massive tombs on its inhospitable shore.

A strong tradition, likely to be factual, is that St Magloire, cousin of St Sampson, brought Christianity to Sark in about the middle of the sixth century. With him came sixty monks and they built an oratory and cells on the site of La Seigneurie, so it is believed. Nearby is an old house, La Moinerie, whose name suggests a monastery.

Sark's history from about 550 to 1550 is somewhat vague. There were times when the French held it and fortified the island. There were periods when pirates made it their stronghold. Doubtless it was

Sark's main street with the island's banks in the background

populated by more agreeable folk during that turbulent millennium, but in wartime an island in an unsettled state could become a menace to its neighbours and to passing shipping.

So it was that in 1563 Helier de Carteret, Seigneur of Le Fief St Ouen, in Jersey, petitioned Queen Elizabeth I for leave to colonise the island with forty fellow-islanders, each of whom would be allotted a *tenement*, in return for which he would pay certain dues to de Carteret and help in the defence of the island. Thus the Fief of Sark came to life (for it was moribund when the island enjoyed no organised government), with Helier as its Seigneur, since the Queen granted him Letters Patent and a Charter. De Carteret's ambitious scheme was successful, the semi-derelict island was put into a state of cultivation, a harbour was made, roads constructed, houses built and an island community established.

Prosperity came to Sark at last and it endured. Successive Seigneurs, first de Carterets, later Le Pelleys and Collings (both families originally from Guernsey) maintained order, thanks to administration by Chief Pleas, the local 'parliament' comprising the 'Tenants' and more recently, members elected by islanders. This form of government continues and works admirably. It must be one of the very rare instances where the feudal system (obviously with modern modifications) is as sound today as it was in the Middle Ages.

In the Napoleonic Wars guns were mounted on Sark's headlands and they survive, rather rusty, dismounted and worthy of more attention than they receive. The Sark Militia, formed originally as part of a feudal service, helped to defend the island and the force remained active until 1880. One of its brass field guns was then melted down and recast as a church bell: swords into ploughshares indeed! Other relics of the militia are a ruined building at L'Eperquerie (once a guard house), the remains of nearby shooting butts, the Arsenal, adjoining the Prison, and some cannon in the grounds of La Seigneurie. In Castle Cornet's militia museum are fine specimens of Sark Militia accoutrements, treasures now in Guernsey, but which might find a home in Sark if and when it has its own museum.

Silver mining in Little Sark transformed this otherwise tranquil island. It was begun during the last century but was short-lived, since output was slight, costs were high and, by 1844, ruin confronted the Sark Mining Company. A major victim was the Seigneur, Ernest Le Pelley, who was obliged to transfer the Seigneurie to Mrs T.G. Collings, the first of the family to control Sark's fortunes. The present Seigneur, Mr Michael Beaumont, is of Collings descent.

Although the mines failed, interest in their working attracted visitors from Guernsey, who found the beauty of Sark more to their liking than an ailing industry at its southern extremity. It is curious to reflect that tourism was born in Little Sark, yet today the vast majority of its day visitors fail to go there. Steam vessels, as well as smaller sailing craft, brought them over in the 1850s and thereafter, hotels were built, the harbour was improved and carriages were bought for their convenience. Since then, the tourist industry has become more and more the key to Sark's prosperity. Farming and fishing are no longer the mainstays of its economy.

During the German Occupation Sark came off comparatively lightly. Of course, there were restrictions and privations, the German presence was felt and some islanders were deported to Germany.

PLACES OF INTEREST IN SARK

Creux Harbour, La Seigneurie gardens (Wednesday and Friday), St Peter's Church, Prison (exterior), Island Hall, windmill (craft shop), lighthouse, Art Gallery (near Mermaid Inn), pottery, Rue Lucas, La Coupée, Silver Mines, Little Sark. (Apart, perhaps, from Little Sark, all these places can be visited during a day visit to the island.)

Other Attractions

During the summer various attractions include a water carnival, the horse show, cattle show, flower and produce shows. Occasional entertainments are provided at the Island Hall, as well as exhibitions, dances and meetings of La Société Sercquiaise, to which the public are welcome.

But food, on the whole, was rather more plentiful than in the other islands, no fortifications disfigured Sark and after World War II its popularity revived quickly and it has increased ever since. It is also esteemed as a place of residence, although the minimum of taxation is in some degree offset by the high price of Sark properties.

Sark's majesty is well appreciated from sea level. To stand on its headlands is rewarding, but only from their feet is their grandeur fully appreciated. For this reason, a boat trip around the island is an unforgetable experience, only to be accomplished in still weather, for the boat enters water-filled caves, an impossibility if the sea is at all turbulent. The launch from Guernsey normally approaches the island via the south of Jethou and the north of Sark and at this point, Le Bec du Nez, she may roll a little in the strong tide.

Sark's east coast is passed and the lack of visible buildings is remarkable. It is, of course, a blessing, since the cliffs' grandeur is unmarred. True, there is the lighthouse at Pointe Robert, but it is different, for it is handsome, interesting and useful. Moreover, it is halfway down the cliff and is not over conspicuous, rather an odd thing to say about a lighthouse! Ahead is **Maseline Harbour**, a concrete structure completed in 1949, when it was opened officially by HRH the Duke of Edinburgh. This was on the occasion of the

Sark's coastline

Queen's visit to Sark, the first monarch to do so. La Maseline lacks the beauty of the highly attractive port of Le Creux, close by, but the latter is dry at low tide, in contrast with its newer neighbour, whose quay is more spacious.

The landing at Maseline is almost at the entrance to a tunnel, hewn through the cliff, through which all must pass, to emerge at the base of the hill leading to the interior. Waiting are small, tractor-drawn buses for those not wishing to walk up the quiet, lovely road, but steep in places. Those wishing to travel by carriage from the harbour, must arrange this beforehand. Before ascending, however, enter another tunnel and gaze at the beauty of **Creux Harbour**. Its quays are of red stone, fishing boats use it and so do small yachts. Occasionally launches and larger craft berth there, according to weather conditions. You may dive and swim in its pellucid waters, paddle from the beach or laze in the sun on its tranquil sea wall. And, for good measure, there is yet another tunnel to see, leading to the beach and far older than its fellows. It was built by Helier de Carteret, the Jerseyman who colonised Sark after it became uninhabited, in 1563. Over his archway, of Jersey granite, is the date of its building: 1588.

Near the top of the harbour hill the buses stop. Here carriages await patrons and they include wagonettes (the most numerous), converted vans and two-wheeled traps. The horses, for the most part, are of the farm variety, although few, if any, are used for agricultural purposes today; they are usually amiable. Equestrians are rather rare in Sark, but cyclists are almost too plentiful, since to hire a cycle is such a good idea that it leads to congestion at times.

At the bus terminus are Aval du Creux Hotel and the Bel Air hostelry, both popular venues. Self-catering accommodation is close by. The main road takes you to the village (just beyond La Collinette crossroads), rather a prosaic collection of buildings, comprising several shops, banks and private dwellings, lining the Avenue, now lacking most of the trees which once adorned it.

 Towards the end of the Avenue a turning right leads to **St Peter's Church**, whose tower and clock are conspicuous. Built in 1820, its architecture is unremarkable, but within there is much charm. There are interesting and sometimes touching memorials, the windows are worth examining and the new cushions and hassocks, with their

Creux Harbour

variety of designs, are extremely attractive. There is an atmosphere of simple reverence in Sark's church, a quality shared in some measure by the graveyards adjoining and opposite.

Close by is the **Island Hall**, of no appeal in style, but an invaluable public building where meetings and entertainments are held and where refreshments may be had. Its neighbour, a small, stone-built school, is also Sark's 'House of Parliament', for here are held meetings of Chief Pleas (quarterly and more often, if needs be) and Court sittings when necessary. The Seneschal is the judge (he also presides at meetings of Chief Pleas) and he is assisted by the Prevôt (Sheriff) and Greffier (Registrar). When these assemblies occur during school hours the children have a holiday. The public are admitted to these meetings, though space is at a premium and it is often a case of 'standing room only'.

St Peter's Church

La Coupée beach

From the Avenue, a short walk westward leads to another school building and the island Prison. This is small and of rather peculiar design, but it suffices Sark's needs, for it is used only for short-term offenders; more serious criminals are sent to Guernsey for trial and punishment. Adjacent is the former Militia Arsenal, now painfully altered from its original simple style. At an angle to the main road is an attractive row of cottages. In one of them Helier de Carteret made his first home. They flank Le Manoir, a gracious house, once La Seigneurie and subsequently the vicarage. Now it is in private hands and the incumbent lives opposite the church.

The road runs westward to the windmill, lacking vanes and looking rather forlorn, partly because the Germans used it for observation purposes. Over the door a stone bears the date of 1571. It has an ornate weather vane, happily spared by the Germans. Helier de Carteret built the mill, and until 1919 it ground the corn of the Seigneur and his tenants. It stands 365ft (111m) above sea level, on the highest point of the island.

(From La Collinette to La Coupée is $1^1/_4$ miles and from La Coupée to the extremity of Little Sark is a mile).

One of the sights of Sark is **La Coupée** and it is easily reached from the village. Past the mill one reaches La Vaurocque crossroads and if one turns left a rather dull road, running south, goes to this remarkable place, having passed some picturesque houses in the valley of Dos d'Ane. Just past the fine residence of Plaisance the road descends through a cutting and suddenly there is an open space, with a drop of about 260ft (79m) on either side of the narrow road, fortunately protected by railings. On the left (east) the drop to the sea is sheer. Opposite, the descent to sandy Grande Grève bay is more gradual and a path takes one to this popular resort. Until 1900 La Coupée was unprotected and crumbly, making it something of a hazard to cross. The present railings were set up by liberating British troops in 1945.

Beyond this cutting (the meaning of *Coupée*) is **Little Sark** and there are many who declare that it is even more becoming than Big Sark, since it is less developed. Certainly its coastline is superb, it has several agreeable buildings and it is far less crowded than its larger neighbour, although 'crowded' is a relative term.

La Coupée, the narrow road connecting Sark and Little Sark

If the road is a little prosaic, its environment is not so. Fields, often occupied by cattle, flank it and, opposite a house named 'Clos de la Pointe', a path runs east and descends steeply to **Le Pot**, a dramatic-looking place on the coast where an attempt to mine copper proved abortive. Bathing here is not recommended, but the scramble down certainly takes one to a wild part of the shore, though the upward climb is to be reckoned with. Not very much further south the road reaches La Sablonnerie Hotel, where refreshments can be bought, as they are in the tea gardens opposite.

Do not fail to look at the picturesque cottages nearby, beyond which the road leads to **Port Gorey**, where at times a *souffleur* may be seen in operation. This lies below the site of the **Silver Mines**, whose ruins in the valley may still be viewed. A good path descends to where the silver was shipped and above survive chimneys and engine house ruins. The area is overgrown and the shafts therefore are very dangerous. A path passes these stone pillars and leads to **Venus's Bath**, a splendid rock pool, deep and excellent for divers, although at high water it is covered. There are signs pointing the way to this famous Sark feature, immortalised by the painter William Toplis. Other rocks accommodate such 'baths', of which the **Pool of Adonis** is the finest. It can be reached, after a long climb, from the cliffs beyond the cottage settlement. From this southern end of Sark the view is outstanding.

One of the drawbacks of going to Little Sark is that, for the most part, one must return by the same route. It can be varied in part, however, by a rather obscure turning right after climbing up from La Coupée, after leaving Little Sark. (Obviously, if one uses this path before crossing the cutting, the turning will be on the left.) It takes one to a way along the summit of the eastern cliffs to **Dixcart Bay** and the pity of it is that there are few such coastal tracks. From it the village can be seen in the near distance.

Soon the track reaches the hotel at Dixcart, situated in sylvan surroundings, at the approach to the lovely Dixcart valley. It is densely wooded, a stream bears the gentle path company, and soon Dixcart Bay is reached, probably the most frequented in Sark, since its approach is the easiest and its charm is beyond dispute. A fine natural arch, impressive cliffs and good bathing are among its favourable aspects.

On the left is the headland of **Pointe Château**, where once stood a small French fort. It is easily reached from the village. From La Collinette crossroads walk south and past the house of La Peigneurie and descend towards Petit Dixcart. A path on the left leads past fields to the Hog's Back, a fine ridge separating the bays of Derrible and Dixcart. Pointe Château is at its extremity, where an old gun lies, one of several on the Sark heights.

Derrible Bay, on the eastern side of Pointe Château, is well worth a visit, even though the path down (and up!) is steep. It is well to follow the track from the Hog's Back, branching eastward (right) on the return from its seaward end. The way descends slightly and continues through a copse. After a short distance a slight trail runs right to the brink of **Le Creux Derrible**. Here tread warily, since the aperture

Natural arch, Dixcart Bay

is unfenced and the drop to sea level is sheer.

This *creux* (surely the finest in the Channel Islands) is about 180ft (55m) from the beach and comprises a shaft, or chimney, rising from a double-entranced cave of some size. It is easily reached from the sandy bay and from its base the prospect upwards is as exciting as that from the rim. Derrible Bay cannot be reached when the tide is high, since the base of the path is then covered. At other times there is a good stretch of sand and caverns to explore. The bathing is good there. Pointe Derrible, east of the bay, is a fine sight, but both difficult and dangerous to visit. Its grandeur is best viewed from a boat. The descent to Derrible Bay begins seaward of a dew pond (a rarity in the islands), which stands at the end of the Hog's Back pathway. Inland, a field path and lane returns to the village.

For a leisurely stroll, go to the **lighthouse**, less than a mile from La Collinette, open to visitors in the afternoon, and worth seeing. From La Collinette walk north along Rue Lucas and turn right towards the Mermaid inn. Just beyond it turn left and then right. The way leads to Pointe Robert and a flight of steps descends to the lighthouse, about halfway down the cliff.

Return up the steps and walk back along the road to a path running north, which leads to La Ville Roussel, a collection of houses of which one or two are ancient. A lane running north-east leads to the cliffs, from which a zigzag path descends to **Grève de la Ville**, a bay best visited in the morning, because of the sunshine it then enjoys. On the right of it is La Chapelle des Mauvres (The Gulls' Chapel), an arched rock shaped somewhat like a chapel. Moorings offshore are used by the hydrofoil, which may also moor off Dixcart.

Northern Sark has a special attraction, inasmuch that its extremity slopes rather gently towards sea level, unlike other parts of the coast. It is easily reached, either via La Seigneurie Road (north of the church) or by a parallel route, Rue du Fort, further east. It is wise to proceed one way and return by the other.

Along Rue du Fort, in about a quarter of a mile, La Tour is reached, a settlement partly enclosed by grassy walls, where once stood an old defence work. Nearby is the farm of Le Fort. The road turns west and joins the Seigneurie Road, and a walk north leads to **L'Eperquerie** common (1 1/4 miles from La Collinette). It is here that the land level declines. A well-defined path on the right runs down to L'Eperquerie landing, above which stand upturned cannon from the East Indiaman *Valentine*, wrecked off Brecqhou in 1781. Boats used to be moored here when fishing was more important than it is today. There is good bathing here.

Ascending the path from the shore, turn right and walk north. Ahead are the remains of the militia butts (more militia remains are the ruined watch-house and mouldering gun at the path's summit) and just before reaching the butts, descend a rather sinister-looking gully, facing west. A short distance down on the right, is the entrance to **Les Boutiques**, caves, second only to Les Gouliots in size and interest. They are not too dark to explore without a torch, thanks to apertures in the walls. Their name, meaning 'stores' or 'shops', is said to be derived from their former use by smugglers, but this is absurd. Free trading in the Channel Islands was not illegal and it is hard to believe that smugglers would use such an awkward place when they were perfectly entitled to use something much better.

The main cave slopes downward; there is a sea cave and two main corridors, the more northerly ending in another gully at sea level. From it one may scramble up to the path leading to Sark's most northerly point, Le Nez. Les Boutiques, like all caves, are best explored at a low spring tide, when conditions are drier than at other times. Beyond Le Nez is a massive grass-covered rock: La Grune, and further on is another: La Corbée du Nez. Le Bec du Nez ends this massive chain of rocks, all of which can be reached at low water.

Returning southwards, one can see a square fort, built by the French when they occupied Sark in the sixteenth century. It stands above L'Eperquerie path and on it an eighteenth-century gun lies in the turf. A little south of the L'Eperquerie track is another, descending to **Les Fontaines Bay**. It is a rocky place and here one finds 'The Fairy Grotto', as artist William Toplis styled it. Looking through two natural arches, when one is in the correct position to appreciate the illusion, the shape of a woman (presumably the fairy) may be seen.

On the return to the top of the cliffs look out for a track leading westward to a seat on the heights. From it one can enjoy one of Sark's most majestic views, extending from Bec du Nez to beyond Brecqhou. It is possible to use a path running along the clifftop for a

Dixcart Bay

short distance in an easterly direction (that is, having returned to the cliffs above Les Fontaines Bay). It is not too severe a scramble to reach the base of Le Creux Belet, a huge gash in the coastline. From there another path goes to Le Fort farm, also accessible from Rue du Fort, the main road. A track by the house runs down to La Banquette landing, via an attractive valley. From the rocks there is bathing for the swimmer and diver. The return to the village is best made via Rue du Fort.

The beautiful house of **La Seigneurie** can be seen at close quarters on Wednesdays and Fridays, when the gardens are open to the public. The residence is not shown. It is easily reached by road and between it and the church are the agreeable houses of Beauvoir and Beau Séjour. Opposite them there is a fine old archway, leading to the Seigneurial grounds, well wooded and extensive. Mellow walls surround the gardens, full of flowers and shrubs. Beside the residence are two former chapels, and one is believed to be medieval. Close by, a path leads to the battery. Here, among more modern ordnance, is a handsome bronze saker, presented to Seigneur Helier de Carteret by Queen Elizabeth I, as its inscription reveals. The gun carriage is modern and was made from timber from HMS *Victory*.

An interesting and becoming dovecote has, for its neighbour, a sturdy tower of stone. At a lower level is a holy well, with traditional associations with St Magloire, the remains of whose religious house are said to be the massive walls adjoining the south façade of La Seigneurie. Beside the well are fishponds (much frequented by ducks) and a stream runs through the tree-filled valley to Port du Moulin.

The house is believed to date from about 1675, when it was known as La Perronerie. In 1730 its owner, Mrs. Suzanne Le Pelley, became Dame de Serk, but preferred to continue living in her own house rather than at Le Manoir, on the road to the mill. So her home became La Seigneurie (both this name and Le Manoir virtually mean 'the residence of a lord of the manor') and it has remained so ever since. It has been added to from time to time and the tower dates from 1854, for use when signalling to Guernsey by the Collings, who had a residence there. From its summit flies the banner of Sark.

From the grounds of La Seigneurie return to the road and walk a few yards north to a turning (left) past the agreeably-sited house, L'Ecluse, and gradually running down the side of the valley to **Port du Moulin** (less than a mile from La Collinette). Before reaching beach level there is a flat area, in which there is an aperture in the massive cliff face. This is 'The Window in the Rock', made in the nineteenth century to enable the Seigneur's men to haul *vraic* from the beach, for use as a fertiliser. To have carried this seaweed up the path manually would have been well nigh impossible and to convey it to land by boat would be a tedious business.

Approach the seaward end of 'The Window' with caution, for the drop to sea level is long and sheer. The aperture reveals a fine 'framed' view of north-western Sark. The flat space adjacent to 'The Window' is thought to have been near the site of the monastic water mill, 'Le Moulin', which gave the bay its name. On the last lap of the descent to the beach, branch left and clamber up (quite easily) to a huge crag, where a broad prospect is your reward. Ahead is the massive rock, **Tintageu** (reminiscent of Cornwall's Tintagel in name and appearance), south is Pegane Bay, north lies Port du Moulin and over the sea are Guernsey, Herm and Jethou. After this pause, make for the beach and notice the splendid natural arch. Through it, when the tide is right, one can reach **Les Autelets**, mighty rocks whose flat tops, perhaps, caused them to be known as 'The Little Altars', although surely 'little' is the wrong word! Kittiwakes nest on these lofty stacks. The beach here is fascinating to examine; but keep an eye on the tide, for the arch is the sole exit, since the cliffs are sheer.

It is rather a long climb up the path to **L'Ecluse**, but before returning to the main road, take the cliff path running north, near L'Ecluse. It is a magnificent viewpoint from which Les Autelets (far below) and a great deal more can be seen. The path itself is pleasant, but is a cul-de-sac, unfortunately, and a return by the same route is unavoidable.

The west coast of Sark is, in the opinion of many, its finest and it can be well surveyed from Longue Pointe, above Havre Gosselin (about a mile from La Collinette). The way to it is easy; just walk past the mill to La Vaurocque crossroads and carry on westward. The lane leads to Beauregard, with its duck pond and seemly collection of buildings. The garden of Petit Beauregard is especially lovely.

L'Eperquerie landing

La Seigneurie gardens

La Seigneurie house

The Battery, La Seigneurie

Beauregard Hotel offers refreshment. Walk along a western way to the Pilcher Monument, a stone obelisk on the cliffs. It commemorates Jeremiah Pilcher, who lost his life with others in 1868 while attempting to cross to Guernsey in wild weather. The view, as ever, is superb, with the islands in the west, Brecqhou in the foreground and below, Havre Gosselin and the Gouliot Caves. Away to the north is Le Nez; southward are more of Sark's glorious cliffs.

Longue Pointe has, at its feet, the **Victor Hugo cave**, best reached by boat. The poet gave it his name when he visited Sark. Of greater interest is **Havre Gosselin**, approached by a zigzag path from the monument and quite a long way down. It is a very small port and is rarely used today, since fishing craft are, for the most part, moored at Les Laches, off Creux Harbour. Vessels from Guernsey only call at this western harbour when weather conditions are adverse on the east coast. When this does happen, passengers are taken off the ship by small boats.

Notice an iron ladder rising from deep water to the cliff path some

The only dovecote on Sark, La Seigneurie

distance above the diminutive quay. It slopes slightly outwards and to climb it is, therefore, somewhat daunting, especially from a tossing boat. Yet this was the only landing place until the quay and steps were added in 1912. Across the inlet is Telegraph Bay, where a cable once ran to Guernsey. One may reach it by a path from the settlement of **La Fregondée** (above the bay), but it is scarcely worth the effort.

La Fregondée itself is attractive, though it was more so when its buildings were thatched. This, of course, applies to all old Sark houses, since thatch is a thing of the past and sometimes unworthy substitutes result. The hamlet can be reached by a track running from Petit Beauregard westwards. It leads to a bold headland, extremely rocky, overlooking the Gouliot Passage, separating Sark from Brecqhou.

Having sat awhile on these great rocks, continue down the path to Sark's finest caves. To do them justice a visit should be made at a low spring tide, when the inner caves can be seen. At other times something of the grandeur of **Les Gouliots** caves (about a mile from La Collinette) can be appreciated, but then so much more remains unvisited. A torch will be a help and, of course, one should dress appropriately, for an exploration entails a degree of scrambling and wading. The reward, rest assured, is an experience unmatched in the Channel Islands.

The first cave to be visited, known as 'The Chimney', leads to the vast main cavern, resembling a huge church in shape and proportions. At one end is the sea, glimpsed through a granite aperture, (one of several, in fact). There are various caverns leading off the main one, the best of which is the Anenome Cave, approached through a 'split arch'. Its walls are completely covered by anenomes of various colours, as well as the curious 'dead men's fingers'. It is all very eerie and perhaps a visit is best made in company and preferably with those who have been there before.

Yet for the sensible explorer there is little to worry about, although the tide must never be forgotten. Even to go to the Gouliots and to proceed no further than the main cave is to behold something so impressive that it will stay in the mind for a long time. The really enterprising may care to swim in some of the caves when tidal conditions permit and this, again, is a novel adventure and devoid of danger if undertaken prudently.

In this area is **Port à la Jument** (less than a mile from La Collinette), a bay reached by a steep track from the lane serving the attractive houses of Le Vieux Port and Le Port. Approach it from Le Clos à Jaon (the crossroads north of St Peter's Church), turn left (west) until the Methodist Church is reached, with an old burial ground adjoining it. Opposite is a lane running to Le Vieux Port and at the end of it is the cliff edge, where the path drops to the bay. The descent is steep but not difficult, and the bathing is good; so the journey is worthwhile. The bay's chief attraction is the vast cave running through La Moie de Mouton and one may swim through it in

Victor Hugo Cave, Sark

safety, provided the sea is calm. The Moie itself is a huge rock mass and, several years ago, a bridge crossed the intervening chasm in order to take sheep to the rock's grassy summit—an unusual grazing place!

BRECQHOU

This island on the west coast is, in a sense, Sark in miniature, for it has the same lovely, lofty cliffs, caves and even a harbour. Moreover, it has a tableland resembling that of its parent, although it lacks the valleys of Sark. Brecqhou is in private ownership and may only be viewed from Sark or the sea. Its area is 160 acres (65ha) and much of it is under cultivation. The residence is modern and extensive.

Once known as Ile des Marchands (Isle of the Le Marchant Family), its proper name suggests a 'break', ie the severance of Brecqhou from Sark. In this 'break' flows the swift current of Le Gouliot, in whose midst stands the stack, La Moie de Gouliot. From Brecqhou's Belème cliff there is an extensive view of Sark's west coast, especially resplendent when lit by sunset. On the island's side facing Guernsey is Le Port, where there is a pier from which a road runs to the house and farm. Across the inlet is a cable crane and goods can be unloaded from a moored boat and conveyed ashore by this aerial method. There is another landing place, Galet de Jacob (Jacob's Ladder), on the north coast of Brecqhou.

Its largest cavern is the Pirates' Cave, well seen from Sark's west coast. An attempt at copper mining was made in the last century, but work was abandoned because of flooding. The island seems to have been inhabited constantly, albeit sparsely. The owner has a seat in Chief Pleas, a privilege granted to Brecqhou's owner when La Dame de Serk (the late Dame Sibyl Hathaway) sold the island in 1929 for £3,000. Today Brecqhou is probably worth £3m.

AROUND SARK BY BOAT

This is an excursion par excellence, but it can only be made in very calm weather, since a boat cannot safely enter a water-filled cave or gully if a swell prevails, and such visits are an integral part of the expedition. Sark's boatmen are few, but it is usually possible to engage one on a trip which will never be forgotten. Take provisions with you, for the excursion will take much of the day.

According to the tide, the boat will leave Creux Harbour or La Maseline and sail north or south. Assume that the boat proceeds south and, almost at once, near Les Laches moorings, is the vast Cathedral Cave. Its neighbour is the gloomy Dungeon Cave, in Petit Derrible Bay. These and other names are, for the most part, unofficial and have been bestowed either by boatmen or their passengers. In every case they are appropriate.

It soon becomes evident that the prospect of Sark from the sea differs greatly from that from the land and the boat glides so close to the shore that details of that magnificent coastline can be enjoyed to the full. There are dozens of caves and they cannot all be mentioned, but the most spectacular receive due attention and, even for those to whom caves have but slight appeal, the sight of giant rocks, natural arches, chasms, inaccessible beaches and congregations of sea birds is surely something worth studying.

Beyond Derrible Bay (whose creux mouth can be seen from the boat) is the **Convanche Chasm**, between Dixcart and La Coupée. It has a soufﬂeur (blow-hole) and a small entrance, leading to a tunnel

Cycling on Sark

in which, in twilight, can be seen deep, clear water. It is an eerie place indeed. Close by is the forsaken bay on the east side of La Coupée.

Le Pot, in Little Sark, presents a rugged appearance and after a pause here the boat leaves the coast temporarily to call at L'Etac de Serk, the great 'haystack' of rock south of the island. It is as easy to land there as it is to scramble to the summit, and what an unusual prospect this provides! Birds haunt this place and its flowers are abundant.

The boat sails back to Little Sark's cliffs, rich in caves and sombre chasms, and passes Port Gorey, where once miners toiled. Traces of the Silver Mines may be spotted, but more pleasing are the flower-decked heights and the massive Moie du Port Gorey, a rock passed by the boat as she reaches Rouge Cane Bay. From the sea the Pool of Adonis is as invisible as the Bath of Venus.

Spectacular rocks lie off La Fontaine Bay, above which some of Little Sark's houses are visible. From the sea its buildings are usually out of sight. Soon the sands of Grande Grève come into view and

Le Manoir, Sark

often there are people leaning on the Coupée railings, watching the boats go by. North of it is Port ès Saies, fine to observe, but impossible to reach, save from the sea. Next is **La Moie des Orgeries**, a massive headland pierced by caverns. Then comes the Victor Hugo cave whose wide mouth the boat may enter.

Havre Gosselin appears next with its landing place, the steep path up to the Pilcher Monument and the impressive cliffs looming above the tiny harbour. The entrances to the Gouliot Caves, the deep, clear water and the majestic succession of heights are the dominant features of this wonderful region. Equally remarkable are the Brecqhou cliffs, well seen from the boat as it explores some of its caverns. One of the best is the **Cormorant Cave**. Normally, the boatmen anchor in these waters for lunch.

The sea entrances to the Gouliots is seen from a fresh angle as the boat sails north to the Moie de Mouton, via the dramatic Gouliot Passage. Its gigantic cave has an enormous square mouth and through this the boat sails into Port à la Jument. Then comes the crag

Beauvoir

of Tintageu, close to Port du Moulin, with its natural arch and sheer cliffs, above which are the woods of La Seigneurie. Les Autelets rear their heads in majesty and their backcloth is the heights of Saignie Bay. Here is a large cave and another *souffleur*. With luck it may be working, but this depends upon the tide.

 After passing the chain of rocks known as Les Sept Moies, the mouths of Les Boutiques come into view. The boat rounds La Pointe du Nez to the cliffs near L'Eperquerie. The Fairy Grotto's charm may be appreciated on the approach to the yawning Creux Belet, on Sark's eastern coast. Its neighbour is the fine Red Cave, with a small mouth and a vast interior. Of special interest is the rock formation creating the impression of a drinking horse.

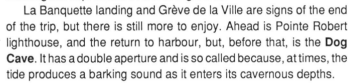 La Banquette landing and Grève de la Ville are signs of the end of the trip, but there is still more to enjoy. Ahead is Pointe Robert lighthouse, and the return to harbour, but, before that, is the **Dog Cave**. It has a double aperture and is so called because, at times, the tide produces a barking sound as it enters its cavernous depths.

USEFUL INFORMATION
FOR VISITORS

HOW TO REACH GUERNSEY

By Sea
Biitish Ohannel Island Ferries
operate from Poole, Dorset,
carrying passengers and cars;

By Air
From several airports with direct
services to the island. They include
London (Heathrow and Gatwick),
Southampton, Bournemouth,
Exeter, Bristol, Leeds Bradford,
Manchester, Norwich, Edinburgh,
Glasgow and Zurich. Enquiries
should be addressed to travel
agents.

Cars
They may be imported to Alderney
by cargo vessel from Guernsey, but
it is more practical to hire them in
Alderney than to take your own.

Cars and other motor vehicles are
prohibited in Sark. In Guernsey
parking spaces are at a premium,
especially in St Peter Port, though
fairly limited accommodation is
available elsewhere.

BUILDINGS AND MUSEUMS

Note: Opening times, where
applicable, are published in *What's
on in Guernsey*, free from the
States Information Bureau, Victoria
Marina, St Peter Port, as well as at
the harbour offices and airport. The
Bureau is always prepared to help
visitors with information required,
likewise the Picquet House, near
the Bus Station. The *Guernsey
Evening Press*, published daily, is
also informative, as is the *Guernsey Globe*.

GUERNSEY
Aquarium
La Vallette, St Peter Port
☎ 23301
Open: daily, 10am-dusk.

Beau Sejour Leisure Centre
Amherst, St Peter Port
☎ 28555
Open: daily, 9am-10.30pm.

Castle Cornet
St Peter Port Harbour
☎ 21657
Open: daily, April-October,
10.30am-5.30pm.

Château des Marais
Grand Bouet, St Peter Port
Always open.

Coach House Gallery
Les Islets,
St Peter-in-the-Wood
☎ 65339
Open: daily in summer.

Folk Museum
Saumarez Park, Castel
☎ 55384
Open: daily, mid-March to early
November, 10am-12.30pm and
2-5.30pm.

Fort Grey Maritime Museum
Rocquaine bay,
Torteval
☎ 65036
Open: daily, May-September,
10.30am-12.30pm and 1.30-5pm.

**Friquet Flower Centre and
Butterfly Farm**
Le Friquet Road, Castel
Open: daily 10am-5pm.

German Occupation Museum
near Forest Church
☎ 38205
Open: daily, 10am-12.30pm and
2-5.30pm.

German Underground Hospital
La Vassalerie Road, St Andrew's
☎ 39100
Open: daily, 10am-12noon and
2-5pm.

Le Gouffre Studio
Le Gouffre, Forest
☎ 65066
Open: daily in summer.

Guernsey Candles
Petites Capelles
Open: daily 9am-5.30pm.

**Guernsey Museum and Art
Gallery**
Candie Gardens, St Peter Port
☎ 26518
Open: daily, 10.30am-5.30pm.

**Guernsey Pottery and
Glassworks**
Les Gigands Road,
St Sampson's
☎ 44282
Open: daily, 10am-5.30pm.

Guernsey Toys
25 Victoria Road, St Peter Port
☎ 23871
Open: daily, 9am-1pm and
1.45-5.15pm.

Guille-Allès Library
Market Street, St Peter Port
☎ 20392
Open: daily, 9.15am-12.30pm and
1.30-5pm.

Hauteville House (Victor Hugo's)
Hauteville, St Peter Port
☎ 21911
Open: daily (not Sundays or Bank Holidays), 10-11.30am and 2-4.30pm.

Koi Farm
Le Marais, Vale

Munson Gallery
Forest Lane, St Peter Port
☎ 21496
Open: daily in summer.

Priaulx Library
Candie Road, St Peter Port
☎ 21998
Open: daily, 10am-5pm.

St Apolline's Chapel
Grande Rue, St Saviour's
Open: daily.

St James' Picture Gallery
Bordage, St Peter Port
☎ 20070 and 22736
Open: daily in summer.

Sausmarez Manor
Sausmarez Road, St Martin's
☎ 35655
Open: late May to end September, weekdays 10.30am-12noon and 2.30-5pm.

Telephone Museum
Le Villocq, Castel
☎ 57904
Open: April-September, Tuesdays and Thursdays 7-9pm.

Le Vau de Monel
Torteval
Open: daily in summer.

Vale Castle
near St Sampson's Harbour
Always open.

La Vallette Underground Military Museum
☎ 22300
Open: daily in summer, 10am-6pm.

Vauxbelets 'Little Chapel'
Open: daily, no fixed times.

Victoria Tower
Monument Gardens, St Peter Port
Open: daily, key at Fire Station opposite.

Botanical gardens
La Villiaze, St Andrew's

ALDERNEY
Court House
To visit, apply to enquiry office downstairs.

Library
Connaught Square
Open: daily.

Museum
High Street
☎ Alderney 3222
Open: daily in summer, 10am-12.30pm.

Pottery
Les Meuriaux
Open: daily.

SARK
Art Gallery
The Mill
Open: daily in summer.

Sark Pottery
Rue Lucas
☎ Sark 2209
Open: daily in summer.

La Seigneurie (gardens only)
Open: Wednesday and Friday,
10am-5pm summer only.

PRINCIPAL ANCIENT MONUMENTS IN GUERNSEY

(for details see index and page
references)

Megaliths (burial chambers or
dolmens)
Creux ès Faies, St Peter-in-the-
  Wood
Delancey Park, St Sampson's
Déhus, Rue des Déhus, Vale
Open: daily 9am-6pm

Les Fouillages, Vale
L'Ancresse sites near La Varde
La Platte Mare, Vale
Rocque qui Sonne, Vale
  schoolyard
Sandy Hook, L'Islet
Sandy Lane, L'Islet
Le Trepied, Perelle
La Varde, Vale

Menhirs (standing stones)
Perron du Roi, Forest
Castel churchyard
Longue Rocque, St Peter-in-the-
  Wood
St Martin's churchyard
St Saviour's churchyard

Promontory Fort
Jerbourg

PARKS AND GARDENS IN GUERNSEY

St Peter Port
Beau Sejour Leisure Centre
Brock Road Gardens, off Grange
  Road
Cambridge Park, near Leisure
  Centre
Candie Gardens, Candie Road
Monument Gardens, near Victoria
  Tower
Sports Centre, Foote's Lane, St
  Peter Port
St Julian's Avenue Gardens
Vallette Gardens, south of harbour

Saumarez Park, Castel
Delancey Park, St Sampson's
Vau de Monel, near Pleinmont
  (National Trust)

Guernsey Gardens Scheme:
During the summer certain gardens
are open to the public in aid of
charities. Details are obtainable
from the Information Bureau,
Victoria Marina, St Peter Port.

SPORT IN GUERNSEY

Badminton
Beau Sejour Leisure Centre
Amherst,
St Peter Port
☎ 28555

Bathing Pools
La Vallette, St Peter Port

Bowls
Indoor Bowls Association
☎ 57100

Guernsey Bowling Club
☎ 46398

Golf
Alderney Golf Club,
Longis Road, Alderney
☎ 2835

Royal Guernsey Golf Club,
L'Ancresse, Vale
☎ 47022

Horse Riding
Rose Dorey
Melrose Farm Stables
% 52151

Guernsey Equestrian Centre
Courtil de Haut, Grandes Capelles,
St Sampson's
☎ 725257

Caroline Jackson
Otterbourne Riding Centre
☎ 63469

Jenny Le Prevost
La Carriére
☎ 49998

Shooting
Full Bore: G. Rich
☎ 724945

Small Bore: P. Syrett
☎ 64786

Pistol Section: G. Le Maitre
☎ 44162

Sub Aqua
Blue Dolphin Sub Aqua Club
Sec: A. Holmes
☎ 55899

Tennis
Beau Sejour Leisure Centre
Amherst, St Peter Port
☎ 28555

King's Leisure Centre
King's Road, St Peter Port
☎ 23366

St Martin's Lawn Tennis Club
Rue du Hurel, St Martin's
☎ 36472

Water Skiing
Horseshoe Ski School
Havelet Bay, St Peter Port

Windsurfing
Guernsey Windsurfing School
Instructor: P. Vivian, Violet Lodge,
Cobo, Castel
☎ 57417

ENTERTAINMENTS

Theatrical and cinema performances are frequently held at Beau
Sejour Leisure Centre and cinema
St Peter Port. There are also floor
shows, discos, opportunities for
ballroom dancing and pub lunches.
Some hotels make their swimming
pools available to the public and
'dip and dine' is popular. Note that
pubs (but not clubs) are closed on
Sundays.

SHOWS

In August, agricultural and
horticultural shows are held at
Sausmarez Manor, St Martin's
(Southern A. & H. Society), Les
Paysans, St Peter-in-the-Wood
(West United A. & H. Society) and
Saumarez Park, Castel (Northern
A. & H. Society). The last includes
the Battle of Flowers. During the
summer flower and produce shows,
horse gymkhanas, fêtes etc take
place. Details are to be found in the
free booklet, *What's on in Guern-
sey*, obtainable at the Information
Bureau and the Picquet House, St
Peter Port.

TRANSPORT

Guernsey
Air UK, Airport, St Peter Port
Aurigny Air Services, South
    Esplanade, St Peter Port
British Channel Island Ferries,
    Jetty, White Rock
Condor Hydrofoils, The Jetty,
    St Peter Port
Customs, Immigration and
    Nationality Dept, The Jetty,
    St Peter Port

Guernseybus, Picquet House,
    South Esplanade, St Peter Port
(All buses return to St Peter Port
from their termini.)
Sark Shipping Office, White Rock,
    St Peter Port
Taxi ranks at Weighbridge and
    Church Square, St Peter Port,
    and Guernsey Airport.

Alderney
Air services with Southampton,
Bournemouth, Dinard, Guernsey,
Jersey and Cherbourg. Access to
Alderney is by air only from
Southampton, Bournemouth,
Guernsey and Jersey.
Railway Station, Braye Gates.

CHURCH INFORMATION FOR GUERNSEY

Anglican
Town Church, Church Square
Holy Trinity, Trinity Square
St John's, Les Amballes
St Stephen's, Les Gravées
St Sampson's, South Side
St Andrew's parish church
St Matthew's, Cobo

St Martin's parish church
St Mary's, L'Islet
St Peter-in-the-Wood parish
    church
St Saviour's parish church
Castel parish church
Forest parish church
Torteval parish church
Vale parish church

Roman Catholic
St Joseph's, Cordier Hill
Notre Dame, Burnt Lane
Our Lady Star of the Sea,
    Delancey
St Sampson's
St Yves, Rue des Landes, Forest

Pentecostal
Eldad, Union Street, St Peter Port
Camp Code, St Sampson's
Vazon

Salvation Army
Clifton, St Peter Port
L'Islet
St Sampson's

Church of Scotland
St Andrew's, Grange Road,
    St Peter Port

Congregational
La Villiaze, St Andrew's

Baptist
Bethanie, St Martin's
Bethel, Landes du Marche, Vale
Bethesda, Forest
Emmanuel Evangelical,
    Grande Rue
St Saviour's
Siloe, St Sampson's
Spurgeon Memorial,
    North Clifton

Methodist

Bordeaux, Vale
Delises, Castel
Capelles, St Sampson's
Camps, Les, St Martin's
Carmel, St Martin's
Ebenezer, Brock Road, St Peter
  Port
Forest, near Le Bourg
Galaad, Castel
Moye, La, Vale
Rohais, (Cobo Road)
St Andrew's
Salem, Vauvert
St Martin's Mission
Torteval
Vale
King's Barn Mission, Castel
Cobo Mission, Castel
First Church of Christ, Scientist,
  Forest Lane, St Peter Port
Friends' Meeting House, Clifton
Jehovah's Witnesses, Kingdom
  Hall, Victoria Avenue,
  St Sampson's

ADDITIONAL INFORMATION FOR GUERNSEY

AA

White Rock, St Peter Port
☎ 22984

Ambulance Service and Hospital

Provided by St John Ambulance,
Rohais, St Peter Port
☎ 725211
They also provides a marine
ambulance and inshore rescue
craft for cliff rescues etc.

Princess Elizabeth Hospital,
La Vauquiedor,
St Peter Port
☎ 725241

Banks (St Peter Port)

Barclays, High Street;
Lloyds, Smith Street;
National Westminster, High Street;
Midland, High Street;
Royal Bank of Scotland, High Street;
Trustee Savings Bank, High Street.
There are several merchant banks
and sub-branches in other parts of
the island.

Guernsey Market

Every Thursday afternoon in
summer this is held in the Market
Square of St Peter Port. It is chiefly
for the benefit of visitors and is both
useful, colourful and entertaining.
Among many items on sale are
traditional Guernsey milk cans,
once in common use of farms and
milk rounds, but now employed
chiefly in the home as hot water
jugs or ornaments.

Libraries

Guille-Allès Library,
Market Street,
St Peter Port

Priaulx Library,
Candie Road,
St Peter Port

Lifeboat

The *Sir William Arnold* (named
after a former Bailiff) is moored in
St Peter Port harbour near the
Royal National Lifeboat Institution's
station.
☎ 720085

Lottery

A Channel Islands lottery is held
fortnightly and a £1 ticket may win
£20,000, or other prizes.

Marinas
Victoria and Albert marinas,
St Peter Port harbour

Beaucette Marina,
Vale.

Newspapers
The *Guernsey Evening Press & Star* is published daily and there is also a weekly edition. The *Guernsey Globe* is published weekly. National newspapers are on sale daily.

One-way Streets — most are in St Peter Port.

Police
Police Headquarters, Le Truchot, St Peter Port
☎ 25111

Post Office
Head Post Office and Philatelic
   Bureau,
Commercial Arcade,
St Peter Port
☎ 26241

RAC
White Rock, St Peter Port
☎ 20822

Radio
Guernsey Radio serves all the islands in the Bailiwick and was established here by the BBC in 1982. It provides local news and features, as well as other programmes.

Speed Limit
35 miles per hour, less in some areas.

Television
In addition to BBC 1 and 2, Channel television (established in 1962) serves the Channel Islands as part of the IBA network and provides a daily local news service as well as occasional features of interest to the islands.

Tourist Information
Tourist Information Bureau, Victoria Marina, St Peter Port.
☎ 23552

Yacht Clubs
Guernsey Yacht Club
Castle Emplacement, St Peter Port
☎ 22838

Royal Channel Islands Yacht Club
North Pier Steps, St Peter Port
☎ 25500

ADDITIONAL INFORMATION FOR ALDERNEY

Alderney Fire Brigade
St Martin's
☎ Alderney 882672

Alderney Police
Queen Elizabeth II Street,
St Anne's
☎ Alderney 882731

Animal Welfare
Alderney Animal Welfare Society,
Val Road.

Banks
Lloyds, Midland, National Westminster and Trustee Savings Banks, all in Victoria Street.

Camping
Only at Saye Farm, overlooking bay: permission in advance from tenant.

Dairy
States dairy. In Val Road.

Dentist
A dental clinic is at the foot of Victoria Street.

Fire Brigade
Volunteer-manned, with station off Marais Square. Summoned by siren.

Gas (bottled)
Alderney Stores and Bunkering, Braye Street.

Hospital
Mignot Memorial Hospital, Crabby. (St John Ambulance available).
☎ Alderney 2822

Library
Island Hall, Royal Connaught Square, Visitors welcome.

Masonry
Temple in Church Street. Visiting Masons welcome.

Medical
Drs S and A Robertson
Ollivier Street, St Anne's
☎ Alderney 2077

Petrol Stations
Alderney Stores and Bunkering Co, Braye.
Alderney Motors, Marais Square, Mouriaux Motors, Les Mouriaux.
Riduna Garage, Newtown.

Police Station
Queen Elizabeth II Street.

Post Office
Victoria Street.

Pottery
Les Mouriaux.

Public Conveniences
Ollivier Street, Marais Square, Butes and Braye (near harbour)
Also at Airport.

Public Telephones
Airport.
Lower High Street (near Clock Tower).
Longis Road (near tall lattice mast at end of High Street).
Braye Harbour.
Whitegates (near Fort Albert).
Sailing Club House, Braye Harbour.

BIBLIOGRAPHY

Alderney, Victor Coysh (Guernsey Press, 1989)

Alderney, Fortress Island, T.X.H. Pantcheff (Phillimore, 1981)

The Channel Islands, A New Study, Victor Coysh (editor) (David & Charles, 1977)

The Channel Islands, an Archaeological Guide, D.E. Johnston (Phillimore, 1981)

The Channel Islands' Landscape, Nigel Jee (Phillimore, 1982)

A Day Out in Herm, Wes Gibbons (Guernsey Herald, 1976)

The Fief of Sark, A.H. Ewen & A.R. de Carteret (Guernsey Press, 1969)

The German Occupation of the Channel Islands, Charles Cruickshank (Oxford, 1975)

The Guernsey House, John McCormack (Phillimore, 1981)

Herm, Our Island Home, Jenny Wood (Hale, 1972)

A History of Guernsey, James Marr (Phillimore, 1982)

Sark, Ken Hawkes (David & Charles, 1977)

INDEX